Continuing Education
and the
Community
College

Continuing Education

Education

and the
Community
College

Jack W. Fuller

Nelson-Hall nh Chicago

Library of Congress Cataloging in Publication Data

Fuller, Jack W.
  Continuing education and the community college.

  Bibliography: p.
  Includes index.
  1. Continuing education.   2. Community colleges.
I. Title.
LC5215.F79   374   78-10905
ISBN 0-88229-371-0

Manufactured in the United States of America

10   9   8   7   6   5   4   3   2   1

Contents

Foreword

Jack Fuller has flung down the challenge to all of us in community, continuing, and adult education to reexamine our principles and rationale related to our specific interests. His hope, expressed openly and sometimes with tongue in cheek, is that we might direct our efforts toward greater agency coordination and perhaps even toward the development of a new concept of education, involving all segments in a concerted attack on societal problems.

The concept may not be as new as I suggest, but Jack Fuller's approach to it is refreshing. He suggests "smart pills," immortality, and even MBOs in a style that is intriguing and scholarly as well.

True, the reader may not find pat answers to perplexing problems and some may even feel slight discomfort, probably objecting to some of the author's conclusions, as I did, but the message is a vital one and relates to a problem that refuses to go away.

The author, with a solid background in adult, community, and continuing education, seems a likely one to comment upon continuing education, and even though the reader may disagree at times, I'm certain that the manner in which the author approaches the problem, his sincerity, and the forcefulness he embraces, will help us to accomplish common goals more resourcefully.

Glenn S. Jensen
Department of Adult Education
and Instructional Services
University of Wyoming

Preface

As the impetus for this book began to take shape, the author was inclined to entitle the text, the concept, and all references throughout as "Conminuing Edvices." The purpose being to illustrate and underscore the similarity and commonality of function and mission between the various aspects of education. The editorial readers, however, found the expression difficult to pronounce and encouraged its deletion. It was the author's contention that for that very reason and its catchiness, its use might help to impress the message of the text upon the reader.

If not earlier than later, the reader will eventually note that the bulk of the content emanates from the author's experience in the community college. This is not to discount the importance of continuing education at other levels in our educational system. Nor does it discredit the applicability of this concept to these levels of education. Apologies are in order if a distortion of reality has been made in any of this. The challenge remains. Namely, to remove the duplication of effort and resources that is gnawing away at the very substance of continuing education. To that end, the author coordinated his publications and research on continuing education into this message.

Continuing Education and the Community College is not an end in itself. It is a suggestion, a challenge, an alternative to what is currently being done. Some of its ideas are speculative, others are surely open to argument. It fails to provide step-by-step procedures as to how continuing education should be implemented. It certainly does not cover all of the possible variables that are encompassed in such a broad concept. It should foster discussion, reexamination, and the like. And that is good.

The book is intended as a mental catalyst for students, professors, and managers of continuing education. It is to be hoped that it will clear the way for some new thought and activity on their part. The book should also serve as an effective and meaningful alternative reading for courses studying the concept of continuing education. For educational managers, it could be a real eye-opener. After reading it, they should have a renewed perspective of continuing education.

And now for some acknowledgments. This book is a product of love! Namely, Glenn Jensen's professional devotion to the mature learner and to teaching. A love that he transmitted to this writer as a student and that will, I hope, be expressed in this book. A book that was conceived and penned in a home full of love: Corky, my supportive wife; Lorae, Jackie, Jason, and Casey, my beautiful children. Without them, the book could have been written. But it just would not have been the same.

A special note of thanks is also extended to the publishers of the various journals listed in the bibliography. They have graciously granted permission for the inclusion of parts or all of some of the articles contained herein. A similar word of appreciation is extended to the editors of Nelson-Hall Incorporated. Their patience and learned guidance steered my professional exuberance into comprehensible reality. The reactions of Terry Whealon, his wife and mine, and Glenn Jensen were equally directive and helpful. A subtle thanks goes to a mother who will never see this book but was always there for consolation when I needed it. And to a father who instigated whatever writing talent I have by making me copy a book, cover-to-cover, in longhand, for bringing home poor grades during my formative years.

Assuredly, none of this could have come to pass without the experiences and opportunity afforded me at one of the most dynamic community colleges around, William Rainey Harper College in Palatine, Illinois.

And last but not least, a special thanks goes to Betty Harmon, Edwyna Rhodes, Mabel Michaels, Donna Santos, and Marilyn Vickers, whose constant typing and perpetual proofreading helped determine the final product.

Introduction

The comedy team of Bud Abbott and Lou Costello earned many a laugh with their routine of "Who's on first?" For those who are too young to remember or so old as to have forgotten, Abbott and Costello would play upon the humor of confusion and frustration generated by a baseball team that had pronouns and phrases for names. The skit would begin with Bud identifying the players for Lou. Lou would become confused with the similiarity between the players' names and the pronouns that Bud would use to refer to the players. It went something like this:

A: I say Who's on first, What's on second, I-Don't-Know's on third . . .
C: Yeah, you know the fellow's name?
A: Yes.
C: Well, who's on first?
A: Yes.
C: I mean the fellow's name.
A: Yes.
C: I mean the guy playing first.
A: Who.
C: The first baseman.
A: Who.
C: The guy playing first.
A: Who is on first!
C: Well what are you asking me for?[1]

It snowballs into a delightful mix-up with Lou, in desperation, finally declaring, "Well, I don't give a damn!" "Oh," says Bud, "He's our shortstop!"

The kind of despair wrought by "Who's on first?" is the genesis for this book and the thrust of *Continuing Education and the Community College*.

The book is this author's answer to the confusion and duplicated time, effort, and money caused by there existing, side by side, such similiar educational functions as:

1. Continuing education
2. Adult education
3. Community services
4. Community education
5. Community development
6. Community schools

Although Ervin Harlacher[2] has ably demonstrated the trouble in discerning between some of the above, the respective missions and purposes of each can be pedagogically defended. But, as Art Burrichter[3] points out, the value of such an exercise is questionable. Indeed, suggests Burrichter, in light of optional management and budgetary considerations, we should probably do away with this senseless and costly charade and seriously consider the possibility of an amalgamation of our resources, clientele, inputs, and outputs. Or as a colleague bluntly and colorfully remarked at a recent professional convention, "There are simply too many horses in the pasture! "

The thesis of this text is to suggest that the saving grace (or grass if you are one of the horses in the pasture) may be to reorganize this segment of education under one common banner. This book is a testimony to that cause in that it demonstrably contends that its content could just as easily be associated with any one or more of the various elements of education that were and are the basis for *Continuing Education and the Community College*.

1 Continuing Education and the Community College

Educational Immortality

For longer than most of us care to remember, educators, in general, have echoed the concept that "learning is a lifelong process." Continuing educators, in particular, can probably and appropriately refer to this concept as their professional genesis and continuing battle cry. But in spite of these realities, the prevailing attitude throughout much of Western society today appears to be that education is still the province of the young. This attitude is further expressed in the opinion that the youth of today are our leaders of tomorrow and that they must be prepared to ably assume this task. Accordingly, the overwhelming proportion of educational budgets, personnel, and facilities are devoted to the achievement of this end. Correspondingly, in this era of economic restraint, the allocations for continuing education are often the first to come under scrutiny.

When and where this occurs, it suggests that the overtures about learning for life are nothing more than shallow rhetoric. If education is for our youth, and if continuing education is one of the first items to be cut from the budget, then what is all of this bellowing about "lifelong learning?"

Continuing educators are in pretty close agreement that mature learners come to an educational situation to:

(1) prepare for or upgrade themselves in their occupational careers;

(2) achieve a given goal, skill, or technique, i.e.,
natural childbirth;

(3) acquire information or knowledge;

(4) fill the personal need for companionship and interrelationship with other people; and

(5) learn new ways to occupy the growing amount of
leisure time.

The gist of this paper is to suggest that there is another
reason that the continuing education student continues to
learn, a reason that transcends the dichotomy between continuing educators and all of their professional brethren. The
reason is, quite simply, the preservation of mankind! A
speaker at a recent education convention reported that:

> . . . if we plot the accumulation of knowledge on an historical
> continuum beginning with the birth of Jesus Christ, we would
> find that the first doubling of knowledge occurs by the year
> 1750; the second in the year 1900; the third in 1950; the fourth
> only ten years later in 1960; and the fifth in the mid 1960's. In
> other words, while it took 1,750 years for man to double his
> knowledge the first time after the birth of Jesus Christ, it only
> took five years for him to similarly double his knowledge from
> 1960 to 1965.

Assuming this fantastic progression of knowledge, it
seems safe to reason that the body of knowledge is probably
now doubling in less than a year's time and soon will be
doubling daily, hourly, and ad infinitum. The statistical
soundness of this account is certainly subject to scrutiny. Who
would deny that it might be less than accurate, especially
when one considers that it purports to measure the sometimes
intangible thing known as knowledge.

In spite of its questionable validity, the statement does
focus much needed attention on a fact that certainly is un-
questioned. Knowledge, in and of the world as we know it, has
grown at an enormously unimaginable rate. And if mankind
is going to attempt to keep up with this knowledge explosion
(as he must if he is to survive), then he will have to develop

many schemes, methods, techniques, and devices to facilitate the learning process. Assuredly, one of these schemes will have to be lifelong learning.

If man is not able to successfully meet the challenge of the knowledge explosion, and all that it entails, he will conceivably not be able to preserve his immediate life system and there really won't be much sense in educating our youth as leaders of tomorrow. If continuing education and lifelong learning do not become prominent mainstays of our social system from this point forward, there very well may not be a tomorrow for our youth to lead. Assuming that this tragedy will be averted, however, and that continuing education and lifelong learning will occupy a fixed position in society, it is imperative that continuing education reexamine its purpose and direction.

Continuing Education: Revised Imperatives

In 1964, a committee of the Adult Education Association,[1] following lengthy study, reported that "If continuing educators are to fulfill their new mission as an 'imperative of our times' the following conditions must be met: (1) there must be a *national perception,* especially on the part of those who control educational policy, of the essential role of continuing education in preventing human obsolescence and in preserving and further developing American society; and (2) there must be a national commitment to provide the resources and moral support necessary for the development of lifelong learning as an integral element of the American way of life."

Recalling the findings of the National Opinion Research Council[2] just a few years earlier, these goals seemed quite in order. At that time, Johnstone and Rivera reported that approximately one-fifth of the total adult United States population was participating in some form of continuing education. With a growing clientele of this magnitude, it was only right that educators, politicians, and the public alike should have been encouraged to set about the task of improving the image and support for continuing education. That this was sound advice can be witnessed by a review of the recent findings of the Carnegie Commission. This study revealed that: "Three-fourths of all U.S. adults between the ages of eighteen and sixty (some eighty million persons) said they want to learn more about something. And one-third of all adults (32 million persons) said they had enrolled during the previous year in some type of learning activity."

This would seem to indicate that, a decade following the Johnstone and Rivera study, the appetite for and level of participation in continuing education had increased significantly. Certainly this revelation was added support for the earlier contention of the Adult Education Association that the national perception of and support of continuing education should be enhanced.

Many colleges, universities, and other educational organizations have recognized this development and have adjusted their programs accordingly.[3] That is to say, they have made provisions to accommodate the growing interest and participation of adults in education. And on occasion, these adjustments have proven financially, as well as professionally, rewarding.[4] But on a less positive note, the support called for twenty years ago has not been as all-encompassing as it should have been if continuing education is to satisfy the imperatives of its times.

In this regard, James Abert[5] makes a good case for expanded funding of programs designed primarily for adults. He points out that our educational system is quick to financially underwrite the education of our youth but somewhat less anxious to similarly support the education of the more mature student. In addition to its lesser monetary support, continuing education has also been found to suffer the following indignities:

1. Low priority in allocation of classroom and office space.
2. Low pay for personnel.
3. Fewer of the privileges and fringe benefits accorded other academic faculty and staff.

    4. Lack of recognition as an equal by others.

    5. Less monetary reimbursement from government agencies than other academic programs.

    6. Little or no opportunities for in-service training.[6]

And in a more recent survey[7] of community colleges throughout the fifty states (thirty-two states responding), it was learned that: (1) less than ten states provide specific funding for continuing education; and (2) the overwhelming majority consider continuing education activities to be "self-supporting."

These findings, coupled with those of a study of continuing education in Michigan community colleges by D. Lundsburg,[8] appear to indicate that the imperatives of continuing education as expressed in the early 1960s are not being met. While the tremendous upsurge in continuing education enrollments would certainly seem to indicate an enhanced national perspective, the literature and studies reveal remnants of the former second-class status of continuing education. And, moreover, it continues to lack financial support equal to its growing importance in today's curricula.

This persisting misconception and maltreatment of continuing education has been the rallying point for critics to label it as "bastard"[9] and to query its existence as "rhetoric or reality?"[10] It is to be hoped that the next decade will witness the refutation of these claims and the establishment of continuing education as a professional peer. And this can probably best be accomplished if continuing education opts for new and revitalized directions rather than continuing to meander along in coerced mediocrity. Perhaps the twenty-six-member Commission on Non-Traditional Study[11] has been the genesis for this sorely needed effort when it suggested the following imperatives:

    1. Education must acquire the perspective that lifetime learning is a reality and a necessity of our times.

    2. Basic, continuing and recurrent education should be strengthened and made more available than at present to the adults of the United States.

3. The scope, nature, and content of educational institutions must be reshaped to accommodate these changing alternatives and clientele.
4. Recent and relevant curricular alternatives and learning delivery systems must be devised, implemented, and adapted to the adult learner.
5. Individual and corporate educational accomplishments must be assessed in accountable terms.

Assuredly, this is not the last word. There are still other imperatives to be uncovered and defined. But the important thing is that the need has been recognized and the initial machinery has been set into action. Now the question remains, "Will these imperatives be satisfied?" The community college is one of the more attractive means to this end.

The Community College

In one of the earliest issues of the *Community Education Journal,* Ervin Harlacher wrote of his concept of the community college. He explained that its role should be to serve as a continuing education center for everyone in the community, a place where every corporate and individual interest and need might be served within the resources available to the college. Today's community college is in keeping with this charge.

Probably the fastest growing and least known phenomenon in education today is the community college. Around the turn of the century, there were only a handful of these institutions. Today, that number is approximately thirteen hundred. The reason for the phenomenal growth of community colleges is due, for the most part, to their comprehensive curriculum. They have something to offer almost every person in the community. Many families have found the community college to be a meaningful way to fill the voids in their lives left by our fast-paced society. And to this extent, the community college might very well be a College for the Whole Family.

A College for the Whole Family

The community college can attract the mother whose family responsibilities have diminished; or a homemaker who is bored with the daily routine; or a father who wants to get ahead on the job; or a son or daughter who is seeking a learning experience not available in other types of schools; or a family that is searching for new ways to do things together and a meaningful way to use increased leisure time.

The typical community college offers a whole host of short noncredit courses, seminars, and workshops for the person who wants to learn but doesn't want the hassle of applications, entrance exams, transcripts, and other trivia usually associated with enrolling in college subjects. But for the person who does want to work toward a bachelor's degree, the community college offers a whole breadth of subjects that are usually found in the first two years of a college or university. Upon completion of these subjects, a person can then transfer on to another school for his bachelor's degree. Many community colleges also cooperate with local colleges and universities to offer junior and senior courses as well as graduate courses on the community college campus. If one's interests are of a vocational or technical nature, the community college also offers a variety of career programs designed to equip the person for the world of work after only one or two years of college training.

In a few instances, community colleges have been known to make the counseling services of their trained and qualified staff available to the public. More often than not, the cost of these counseling services is commensurate with a person's ability to pay and consequently much less than similar counseling and testing services performed by private firms.

Community colleges also make their recreational facilities available to the public. An afternoon or evening of individual exercise or a game of volleyball or basketball with the family might be just the thing to get back in shape. In addition to physical exercise, conmunity colleges usually offer a cultural series, including guest speakers, films, and art shows, and many other cultural pursuits. Community colleges can also provide both meeting rooms and luncheon facilities at a reasonable price for clubs and organizations.

Without a doubt, the community college has a lot to offer every citizen and family within the community. In fact, community colleges have so much to offer that they have often been accused of trying to be too many things for too many people. But this something-for-all attitude is in keeping with the philosophy of the comprehensive community college.

Following the founding of the first junior college around the turn of the century, the major thrust of the two-year college was to provide the first two years toward a bachelor's degree. During these developmental years, the two-year colleges were appropriately called junior colleges. Today, however, the curriculum of the two-year college consists of more than just college transfer programs; it is aimed at every citizen in the community. In addition to college subjects, community colleges now offer a whole host of vocational/technical career programs and continuing education options. For this reason, the bulk of the two-year colleges are no longer called junior colleges, but are rightfully called community colleges. And as community colleges, they offer the individual and the family more than just a wide range of educational, recreational, and cultural opportunities.

One of the most attractive features of the community college is its cost to the student. The tuition rarely exceeds $30 per course. Some colleges are tuition free. With the rising costs of higher education, this low tuition rate is one big reason why so many families are turning to the community college to ease the educational strain on their pocketbooks. By not going away to school, as much as $5,000 can be saved by earning the first two years of a bachelor's degree at the local community college. In spite of the low tuition, some community college students still need monetary assistance. Where this is the case, the community college offers many scholarships, grants, student jobs, and low-interest loans. In fact, on many community college campuses as many as half of the students are receiving some form of financial assistance.

But the matter of money is hardly a concern when a member of the family decides to attend a cultural event or use the recreational facilities of the local community college. Both of these opportunities are usually available for a nominal fee. Charges for the use of meeting rooms and dining services are reasonable but will vary according to the circumstances. In addition to being well within the financial means of families, community colleges are usually within easy commuting distance of the home.

One of the driving forces behind the community college phenomenon is that it should provide the vehicle for everyone and anyone to continue their education throughout life. On the impetus of this driving force, a growing number of states have developed and implemented a master plan for higher education that provides for the creation of a community college within the reach of every citizen in the state. To this end, attending the local community college is often as easy as going to the nearest shopping center or golf course. Upon arrival, it is just as convenient to enroll in classes or arrange for the use of facilities. In fact, in many community colleges a person can make his arrangements with the school by telephone or by mail without ever having to visit the campus. Moreover, the student need not have to worry about being accepted by the college. Conmunity colleges are well known for their open-door admissions policy.

Simply stated, the open-door admissions policy means that anyone who can benefit from community college instruction will not be refused admission to the college. Although entrance exams might be required, they are used solely for placement and counseling purposes and not as a criteria for judging acceptance or refusal of admission to the college. Some people have criticized the open-door policy on the grounds that it lowers the standards of the college by attracting students of lesser ability who must, in turn, be serviced by second-rate academic programs and remedial and vocational instruction. While there is a grain of truth to this criticism, a review of the facts sheds doubt upon its credibility.

Insofar as the academic program is concerned, studies

have overwhelmingly reported that, after a brief period of adjustment, upper classmen at four-year colleges and universities do not perform significantly differently from each other on the basis of where they got their first two years of college education. Regarding remedial instruction, it is entirely within the philosophy of the community college to provide an opportunity for everyone in the community to become whatever he or she is capable of becoming—regardless of past school performance or the length of time out of school. If a person wants to better himself through education, a community college is not going to turn that person away because he needs to learn or refresh skills and knowledge. Vocational education can hardly be considered a degrading aspect of the community college curriculum. In this day and age when Ph.D.s are begging for work and the plumber is getting $25 an hour for his services, it makes a lot of sense for a person to enroll in vocational courses that insure him a good, paying job at graduation.

In the last analysis, the fact of the matter is that there is probably no other institution in society which can so conveniently provide all of these things under one roof to such a broad range of people at such a reasonable price. This fact alone is quite a testimony to the community college and what it has to offer every member of the family. And it is probably because of this comprehensiveness, that it attracts the type of person that it does.

Community colleges boast a student population that is well represented by students who are in their forties, fifties, and sixties. One college of ten thousand students recently reported that it had more than four hundred students over the age of forty-five. Not only is the average community college student a mature person, he also tends to be gainfully employed. Some studies have indicated that as many as 60 to 80 percent of the full-time students are gainfully employed, while almost all of the part-time students are occupied with a full-time job or family responsibilities.

There should be little doubt that the community college is not something to be ignored. If families have not taken advantage of the year-round educational, cultural, and recreational opportunities at the local community college, they can hardly cite quality, cost, convenience, or embarrassment as a reason. Community colleges offer high-caliber programs for people of all ages, interests, and means—right in their own backyards. And to this end, they could be rightfully categorized as A College for the Whole Family.

That the community college has something that could appeal to all of the members of a typical American family is indicated by its comprehensive curriculum. But while the family is usually satisfied, the student is occasionally disillusioned. Disillusioned to find that the community college is sometimes not all that it is cracked up to be. For example, consider this essay called "The Community College Image," by a recent graduate of a community college education program.

> "Upon completing my doctoral studies in community college education, I embarked upon my career with enthusiasm and the impression that the concept of the community college was, by now, an established and accepted level of our educational system. But I was soon inclined to suspect elements of the contrary. To be sure, the community college had made an indelible mark in our educational annals. But after a few years as a community college administrator and innumerable contacts and exchanges with educators at all levels and the lay public, I was made brashly aware that the community college had a long way to go before it would be viewed in the proper perspective.
>
> "In retrospect, the two-year college had been in existence for almost three-quarters of a century and was yet to distinguish itself with the label of a community college. At its inception, the two-year college was looked upon as a feeble extension of the high school curriculum and/or an inferior substitute for the first two years of a four-year college education. Since its inception, however, the two-year college has broadened its role to include vocational/technical career programs and continuing education offerings. Moreover, it has refined its developmental and college transfer curricula to a state that is unrivaled by almost any high school district or four-year college or university.
>
> "In spite of these important and far-reaching developments, however, the image of the community college has apparently not changed in the eyes of many high school and college educators. Their perception of the community college is aligned

with the past and not today. Accordingly, their everyday professional performances related to the community college only propagates this antiquated misconception. Some students are "counseled" with the impression that four-year colleges are "better if you're going on" or that community colleges are primarily a remedial or vocational education institution.

"Further, many four-year college administrators and teachers continue to 'look down' upon their partners in the educational system by not accepting certain courses as transferable or else requiring students to successfully 'challenge' a course they have already satisfactorily completed at the community college. What is even worse, many community college faculty and staff see themselves solely as partners in a four-year college process and not also as participants in a unique aspect of the educational system with equal emphasis upon the continuing education and the occupational student. Often the college faculty has a limited concept of the continuing education program and label it as 'mickey mouse' or 'basket-weaving.'

"It's time that high school and college educators become more totally aware of the community college. It's time that community college faculty and staff become better acquainted with the community college concept. The community college has come too far to have its very fiber threatened by the profession which serves it. If the community college is to really come into its own, then its proper image must be protected from the attacks of ignorant professionals and perpetuated and promoted by a corps of educators especially oriented in the community college concept."

The bitterness, disappointment, and anxieties of this young essayist are obvious. He would, no doubt, subscribe to the position that "If the community college is truly a community oriented and community-based institution as its proponents would contend, then it would find no better starting point in properly projecting its image than in its continuing education element." He would probably also agree, however, that this projected avenue of success is not without its difficulties.

The Bastard of Community College Education

Webster defines "bastard" as something inferior. In the early seventies, a study was conducted to verify the hypothesis that the continuing education dimension[12] was of an inferior status to college transfer programs in community colleges. Harlacher[13] among others pointed out that continuing education was a distinct and major function of the community college. In testimony of the importance of the continuing education function, Thornton[14] advised that the scope and adequacy of these services determined whether or not a college even merits the title of "community" college. There was reason to believe, however, that these attributes were not typically manifested in the so-called community colleges of today.

Armond Festine,[15] for instance, reported from his study of the community colleges of the State of New York that the colleges were not recognizing the importance of continuing education. In support of Festine's findings, the well-known adult educator, Glenn Jensen,[16] warned that community colleges would be well advised to pay more attention to their continuing education function. Based on the brief experience of this writer, the comments of his colleagues, and the under-the-breath asides overheard at professional meetings and conventions, there was reason to believe that Festine's findings might apply outside the State of New York and that Jensen's warnings had gone unheeded. Perhaps Blocker, Plummer, and Richardson's[17] limited treatment of the continuing education mission within the community college system was indicative of a secondary role. Perhaps the continuing education function was indeed a bastard in community college education.

The Survey

In an attempt to vindicate the reputation of continuing education, this author conducted a survey of continuing education directors or their equivalent in a random sample of two hundred community colleges throughout the United States. The survey was designed to measure the directors' perception of continuing education in their respective colleges. One hundred and one usable questionnaires were returned. The number was later reduced to one hundred to facilitate calculations.

There were fifteen items on the questionnaire. In the first five items of the questionnaire, the respondents were asked to rank in descending order of importance from one hundred to four hundred the four community college programs, i.e., college transfer, continuing education, vocational/technical, and student services, with regard to the following items:

1. Priority in assignment of classroom space.
2. Priority in assignment of office space.
3. Difficulties in starting a new program.
4. Salary levels.
5. Number (head count) of students enrolled (served).

The bar chart representing the responses to questions number one and number two revealed that continuing education ranked a distant fourth in the allocation of classroom and office space, far behind the college transfer program. Of course, this difference might be warranted. For example, the respective educational needs of a given community might dictate an emphasis of the college transfer program. On the other hand, this difference might very well indicate an allegiance to the "junior college" concept rather than the contemporary "community college" philosophy.

Figure 1–1

Allocation of Classroom Space—Question No. 1

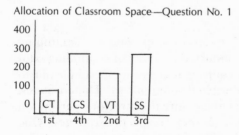

Allocation of Office Space—Question No. 2

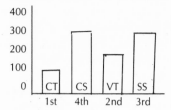

CT = College transfer
CS = Community services (Continuing Education)
VT = Vocational/technical
SS = Student services

The bar chart for question number three showed that there was little difference between the four programs in terms of hurdles encountered in embarking on a new program. In a relevant aside, however, it was interesting to note that vocational/technical programs encountered the most difficulties. Assuredly, the relatively higher cost of establishing many new vocational programs was probably a major factor

Figure 1–2

New Program Hurdles Encountered—Question No. 3

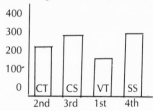

CT = College transfer
CS = Community services
VT = Vocational/technical
SS = Student services

underlying this finding. Another reason for the number of new program hurdles encountered by technical programs was that they probably still bear the stigma of non-college-transfer programs. If so, it was further testimony to the contention that community colleges tend to place an emphasis on the college transfer aspect.

In question number four, the respondents were asked to rank the salaries paid to the faculty and staff of the four programs. As the appropriate bar chart indicates, the salaries of continuing education personnel ranked way behind those of college transfer programs. A promising note lay in the relatively high ranking of salaries paid to the faculty and staff of vocational/technical programs. This was further evidence, perhaps, that career programs are beginning to assume more of the recognition to which they are entitled. Less promising were the salaries paid to student personnel workers. Their salaries ranked close to last, just above those of continuing education personnel.

In somewhat of a surprise, the bar chart for question number five revealed that the greatest number of students was served by the college transfer program, with vocational/technical programs running a close second. To hear continuing educators boast their way about professional meetings and conventions, one would think that they were far above other community college programs in terms of enrollment. It was encouraging to note that vocational/technical programs have apparently begun to shed some of their stigma and to attract a growing number of students. It was disappointing to note that student services, the program that should be ideally reaching all of the students, was apparently reaching the least.

In the remaining items of the questionnaire, the respondents marked a Yes or No response. Because the sample size used was 100, it was easy to convert these responses to percentages. In questions number six, eight, and fourteen, about one-half of the continuing education directors responded that there was not an accurate perception of the community services function at their college. A similar number felt that their institution did not properly acknowledge community

Figure 1–3

Salary Levels—Question No. 4

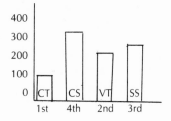

Headcount Enrollment—Question No. 5

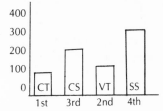

CT = College transfer
CS = Community services
VT = Vocational/technical
SS = Student services

services. Fifty percent of these directors also indicated that their faculty did not receive privileges comparable to the regular full-time faculty.

6. Accurate Perception of Community Services: *YES* 48% *NO* 52%

8. Proper Recognition Accorded Community Services: *YES* 46% *NO* 54%

14. Comparable Faculty Privileges for Community Services: *YES* 50% *NO* 50%

In about half of the colleges surveyed, the faculty and staff of the college transfer, vocational/technical, and student services programs were reported to have an accurate perception of continuing education; about half of the community colleges reportedly accorded the continuing education program the proper recognition; and exactly 50 percent of the colleges reportedly provided the continuing education faculty and staff the same privileges (parking, office space, bookstore discounts, and so on) given to personnel in the other three programs. With nothing more than a fleeting glance, the balance of a fifty/fifty response would masquerade the fact that 50 percent of the respondents felt that their colleges did not have the proper perception of continuing education nor did they accord it complete recognition. Probably because it was not properly recognized, 50 percent of the colleges apparently do not provide the continuing education faculty and staff with the same privileges given other personnel—a case of second class citizenship if there ever was one!

The directors of continuing education indicated that 68 percent of the faculty and staff of the other three programs did not perceive the continuing education function as a threat for space, students, or funds. This response might be attributed to a well concealed commitment to the comprehensive community college concept. But because the gist of this study and a review of the literature indicated otherwise, it appeared more prudent to conclude that community college personnel tended to have a less than minimal understanding of continuing education and accorded it a corresponding amount of recognition. Because this was probably the case, there was little reason for the college transfer division to perceive continuing education programs as a competitor for space, students, or money. After all, did Goliath fear David?

In further support of its bastard image, 80 percent of the continuing education directors indicated in question number ten that their programs received less monetary reimbursement than the other college programs. Clearly, politicians and educators were providing only token support and lip service to the principle of lifelong learning and the importance of the role of continuing education in the community college system of education. Perhaps the meager financial support explained why 99 percent of the respondents stated in question number eleven that there was no in-service education program for continuing education faculty and staff.

On the other hand, in question number twelve, it was revealed that 65 percent of the colleges had in-service education programs for the personnel of the other three programs. Evidently continuing education was not important enough to warrant a well trained, up-to-date corps of professionals.

Nevertheless, question number thirteen indicated that 75 percent of the colleges expected the same standards of program quality from continuing education as was expected of the other three programs. Providing less funding and less training but expecting comparable quality of continuing education is a literally untenable position.

As might be expected, 85 percent of the continuing education faculty and staff were classified as part-time. Fifteen percent of the personnel of the other programs were classified as part-time (question number fifteen). This is justifiable. The broad range of content and the extreme amount of flexibility demanded by a continuing education program almost precludes the possibility of finding full-time personnel with multiple capabilities to staff a complete and varied program. On the other hand, the 15 percent of part-time people employed in programs other than continuing education reduces the need for additional full-time faculty contracts and at the same time offers a chance for students to be exposed to practicing engineers, businessmen, etc. in a classroom situation.

And as if in crowning glory unto the kingdom of bastardom, let it be known that fully 40 percent of the respondents revealed that their college did not have physical adaptations to their buildings for mature students.

As any practitioner of continuing education knows, the bulk of his students are adults. The adult physiological development often requires better acoustics, stronger lighting, fewer stairs to climb, and less distance to the parking lot. The community college that does not make these and other adjustments to its physical plant is not thinking of the adult student. But then again, here is only one more reason why today's two-year colleges are always in quest of the "community college" designation—they are designed primarily with the younger, college transfer student in mind and pay only lip service to the broader college community clientele, inclusive of the adult.

This study was not performed with experimental rigor. Its validity was open to question. But whatever can be said of its findings, there was no denying the fact that it revealed some very serious areas of concern to community college educators. It pointed out that the area of continuing education in the community college was not a full-fledged partner of the college transfer program. At this point in its development, continuing education was very much like a bastard in community-college education.

2

Foundations of Continuing Education

The basic elements of a continuing education program are common, regardless of whether you call it continuing education or community education, and regardless of its subject. These common elements would certainly include among other things: (1) elements of establishing the program; (2) staff development; (3) methodology; (4) management; and (5) facilities.

In and of themselves, each of these is substantive enough to warrant an entire text. But I hope the following will be illustration enough of each of these elements. In keeping with the thesis of this text, they should be viewed and evaluated in terms of their applicability throughout the entire spectrum of continuing education.

Elements for Establishing a Continuing Education Program

A Challenge

With the rapid growth of continuing education throughout the United States, there has arisen a corresponding growth in the need for some general guidelines in establishing these programs. While this need most certainly exists, little has been done to meet it. Some professionals who are involved in this matter have tackled this problem with the trial-and-error approach. Admittedly, this approach has some merit if one accepts the premise that each community and each educational institution is different; hence, each institution and each community might require a different approach or at least some variation from a general set of guidelines. Nevertheless, there should be some point of reference, some base of deviation to which the programmer of continuing education may refer.

The following guidelines for establishing a continuing education program are not offered as the final answer. Rather, they are an invitation to others to improve upon them. It is to be hoped that this account and the response of its critics will form the nucleus for a comprehensive set of guidelines for establishing a continuing education program.

The Guidelines

The starting point for all continuing education programs is, of course, to determine the needs and wants of the population to be served. Once identified, they become the basis for the courses, classes, lectures, and workshops to be offered. Formal and informal surveys of civic organizations, fraternal clubs, business and labor groups, and faculty and staff are one way of determining what the community wants or needs in the way of continuing education. The professional literature of continuing education is another source of ideas for programs and courses. Frequently, a person with a given knowledge approaches the programmer and persuades him that his idea for a class would "go" if it were scheduled. Radio, television, newspapers, and magazines provide the programmer with current trends that might be the impetus for additional offerings. Continuing education advisory committees representing broad ranges of the community spectrum are also valuable sources of information for programmers. But even the strongest request should be examined and weighed closely. Quite often the professional greed to have a larger program and to add a class for some students who could get the same service a few miles away can lead to expensive and senseless duplication. A gentlemen's agreement or perhaps a well-defined quasi-contract stipulating the intent not to duplicate courses or programs between overlapping service areas enhances the success of respective programs.

But in some cases, this option appears ignored or out of reach. For example, one Midwestern university flies professors more than one hundred miles almost daily to one of the largest metropolitan areas in the United States. That one of the ten or more universities in that city couldn't offer the classes, or that of the five million or more population, qualified instructors cannot be found nearby, is difficult to comprehend. Just as incomprehensible is the western university which flies its professors over two other major state universities enroute to the opposite end of the state to offer a program available from another school much closer.

Almost as important as identifying the need and programming accordingly is promoting the program. Even the most well-planned program will go unattended and never be successful if it is not well-advertised. The programmer should exhaust every means at his disposal to publicize his program. Having a list and description of the courses reproduced in an attractive manner is a necessity. Mailing this publication to every resident in the service area is most desirable. Placing this list in places of business that are frequented by the clientele has proven successful. Inserting leaflets with the monthly utility bills or Sunday newspaper has been done by some programmers. Short spots on radio or television are feasible. Contacting special-interest groups in the community and sending them a list of offerings that are pertinent to them might be a good idea. These suggestions are only a few of the possibilities for promoting a continuing education program. Certainly, the creative programmer can think of many more.

Once the program has been determined and while it is being promoted, a continuing education programmer should establish the competency level that will be required of his instructors and begin the staffing process. In some cases, a state board of agency has predetermined teacher qualifications. While some state boards and agencies set forth specific requirements for continuing education teachers, the greatest number appear to be satisfied with simply requiring that they be competent. Usually the matter of determining competency is left in the hands of the interviewer.

An important and unavoidable part of the staffing process involves determining teacher salaries, fringe benefits, and class schedules. With regard to these matters, continuing education teachers are an unusual breed. They are usually part-time moonlighters who are supplementing their salary from a full-time job, and their availability to teach is, of course, dictated by the demands of their regular occupation. Courses may have to be scheduled on certain nights or times and even at special locations if they are to be taught at all. Except for the fulfillment of the ambition of continuing education instructors to teach, fringe benefits for them are virtually nonexistent. Some would contend that this practice (as compared to all the benefits for full-time faculty) could conceivably be associated with legal concerns like discrimination, equal opportunity, due process, and property right. In fact, at this writing, there is a strong movement in the state of California by part-time faculty for a proportionate receipt of full-time faculty benefits. Lest these concerns manifest themselves into substantive issues, the programmers of continuing education would do well to be alert to their development and sensitive to personnel situations that might hasten their arrival.

In arriving at the salary for continuing education teachers, it is suggested that paying everybody at the same rate is most equitable and administratively expedient. Yet, others would contend that different instructors might justifiably deserve different salaries. A programmer should be prepared to expect a lawyer or physician to demand a higher salary to teach a class than the yoga or astrology teacher. But the continuing education administrator often does not have the bargaining skills or authority, not to mention the lack of fiscal wherewithal and power to deal with his faculty in this latitude. Whatever his decisions with regard to faculty, salaries, benefits, and schedules, the continuing education programmer should see that they are explicitly set forth in a contract and that this document and its contents are agreed to and signed by each part-time faculty member.

Important addenda to this contract that the programmer might want to consider are (1) that the class will be offered in the place designated by the employer, and (2) that the class and contract are cancelled if a minimum number of students do not enroll by the first or second meeting. In the latter case, the contract should specify the terms of payment, if any, should a class not materialize.

Another matter for the programmer to consider is the number and kinds of courses that he can offer in terms of his budget. This matter becomes increasingly difficult when the variables of tuition and government reimbursement are inserted into the budgetary estimate. Whereas it is impossible to predict the number of students who will enroll in a course and hence the amount of funds that the budget will receive from tuition and per capita reimbursements, the programmer must allow for monetary profits in some courses and monetary losses in others. The two may balance out. Faster than most of us would have it, "self-supporting" is becoming the byword of continuing education.

Any continuing education program must note a few items peculiar to the mature learner. Because of their myriad social obligations, mature learners are more likely to enroll in and "stay with" a course that is relatively short in duration. The acceptable range of duration for a continuing education course is probably about six to ten weeks. Because of the students' matured sociopsychological makeup, the programmer should encourage instructors not to use grades and tests for pass-fail purposes in the classes. The programmer should also encourage instructors to never lecture more than twenty minutes; rather, they should exploit the techniques of group discussion, demonstration, field trips, and so on. Finally, because money plays such an important role in our society, the programmer should keep his tuition rates as low as possible.

Evaluation and follow-up are musts in a continuing education program. Evaluating each class in the program not only provides the programmer with the information he needs to improve the quality of his program but it also enables him to get ideas for additional courses and programs. Consequently, the programmer is behooved to devise a system of evaluating each of his classes and programs on an ongoing basis. A similarly profitable parallel can be drawn for evaluating the continuing education faculty and staff. Based on the findings of this evaluation process, in-service programs can be developed and implemented.

An In-Service Program
for Continuing Education Faculty

The subject and existence of in-service education programs is nothing new on the educational scene. They have existed for years for full-time faculty and staff. Word of mouth has it that on occasion they have even been available for some part-time faculty and staff. Research does not reveal, however, the recorded attempts of many such programs for the continuing education teacher. Perhaps this research void is attributable to happenstance. Which is simply to say that in all the years of continuing education, an educator has never thought of providing an in-service education program for continuing education faculty. And if it had been thought of before, it had not been implemented. And if it had been implemented, it had obviously not been recorded for posterity. Because all of this sounds highly unlikely, it seems safer to reason that this was simply another example of the place of continuing education in the eyes of the "powers that be" in education to date. It has probably been part of their philosophy and practice not to allocate funds for in-service education programs for the part-time, moonlighting teachers.

One community college took a significant step towards correcting this problem. In an attempt to maintain a staff who were always in touch with their part-time profession, the college implemented an in-service education program, tailored to suit their unique relationship to the school and the student. In so doing, it was necessary to devise a program that required minimal attendance and responsibilities in order to accommodate the varying full-time work schedules of the teachers involved. After much thought and consideration, it was decided that the most practical, efficient, and fruitful approach might be a self-instruction system. By pursuing this means of in-service education, the teacher could progress at his or her own pace and at times that were most accommodating to his or her regular work schedule. But before a definite commitment was made to this approach, it was decided to gather evidence of its merit. Accordingly, at William Rainey Harper College, Palatine, Illinois, a pilot project was implemented for one year beginning in the fall of 1970.

The Experiment

A pilot group of fifteen continuing education teachers was randomly chosen to participate in the in-service education program. The profile of the pilot group revealed that the average age was thirty-two, with three years of college education. On the average, the seven males and eight females had six years of work experience, of which three were in teaching.

The participants in the experiment were excused from all other in-service responsibilities and were asked to devote their efforts solely to the pilot program , which consisted of a self-instruction booklet of the "instruction-by-objectives" approach to teaching. The booklet was about two hundred pages in length. Upon completion of the booklet (program), the teachers were to have planned their respective courses by the instruction-by-objectives approach. The teachers were asked to complete the program by the end of the fall semester and to use the new approach in teaching their courses during the spring semester.

The experiment began with a one-hour orientation breakfast at which a brief explanation of instruction-by-objectives was imparted. Following the explanation, a short exercise in programmed instruction was completed by all to acquaint them with this technique of teaching. A question and answer period followed. At the close of the orientation, the teachers were encouraged to consult with their supervisor throughout the year as the need arose. Additional meetings of the pilot group were not scheduled. They did, however, receive periodic memorandums reminding them of their self-instruction, in-service education responsibilities.

At the completion of the pilot study, a follow-up survey was administered to the participants. The purpose of the survey was to measure the response to the self-instruction system of in-service education. Three teachers did not complete the survey or the program because their classes were cancelled for insufficient enrollment. These teachers felt no commitment to participate in the in-service education program. Of the twelve who did participate in the program, ten completed planning their courses by the instruction-by-objectives approach. In the writer's evaluation of the instruction-by-objectives materials that were completed, it was estimated that there was much room for improvement. Nevertheless, they were comparable in quality to course outlines that were planned by the objectives approach and that were not related to this experiment.

In terms of professional development, five teachers felt that the program was of *Great Benefit* and seven that it was of *Some Benefit*. None of the teachers felt that the program was of *No Benefit*. Five members of the pilot group responded that the program was *Challenging*, and six, that it was *Somewhat Challenging;* one teacher responded that the program was *Not Challenging*. Eleven participants in the experiment indicated that the self-programmed instruction was *Easily Comprehended* and one that it was *Difficult to Comprehend;* five members of the group reported that the program was *Interesting* and another five reported that it was *Somewhat Interesting*. Two teachers rated the program *Boring*.

Although the program did not rate very high on the interest factor, six teachers rated it as *Informative* and the remaining six *Somewhat Informative*. Seven of the respondents evaluated the orientation session as *Good* and four as *Average*. The only recurring criticism was that not enough supportive meetings were held throughout the year to complement self-service instruction.

The findings of this pilot study provided some strong suggestions for improving the in-service education program at this community college, and although the project was not repeated in subsequent years, it firmly embedded programmed instruction and instruction-by-objectives as potential in-service education tools for part-time community college faculty. For example, most of the teachers reported that the self-instruction format was comprehensible and informative. The program received its lowest rating on the items of challenge, interest, and frequence of supportive meetings. Each of the negative features could easily be improved by a simple rewriting of the program and increasing the frequency of meetings. As an aside, it would appear that any self-instruction program that is worth its salt should be kept relevant and up-to-date by constant revision anyhow.

This study was only a pilot project and, therefore, was very limited in scope and experimental rigor. If it is to provide continuing education with a basis or model for the planning and development of future in-service education programs, it must expand the sample size and be submitted to an exacting statistical measure. Moreover, it must be compared to other types of in-service education programs so that the factors of interest and challenge can be viewed in the proper perspective.

Admittedly, the self-instruction program was not without flaw. While it did show some promise, it was obviously in need of improvement. Accordingly, it could be rewritten to make it more challenging. Videotapes on teaching techniques could be added in an attempt to make it more interesting. Finally, additional meetings could be planned throughout the year in addition to the orientation session. Quite possibly, these adjustments would make the program a viable means of providing in-service education programs for part-time teachers. Given these changes and the potential success of the program, the same performance-based concept could and should apply throughout the entire continuing education program.

Continuing Education by Objectives

One of the most meaningful ideas to come upon the educational scene in recent years has been that of behavioral objectives. The thrust of this movement has been to encourage administrators and teachers to perform their duties with a systematic approach toward given ends. In capsule, this means that they will define the:

1. Objectives to be accomplished;
2. Maximum time period allotted to the accomplishment of each objective;
3. Criteria for minimal achievement of the objective.

At face value, it would appear that all of this is nothing new and actually has always been the mode of operation for organized institutions and individuals. But this assumption should not go unqualified. True, an efficient operation has probably always been the result of good planning. But all too often, the plan took the form of a verbal commitment that was highly subject to dissipation and the unpredictable course of events that might occur between the beginning and end of the semester. In an ideal objective-operated situation, the objectives are set down on paper and periodically reviewed for progress.

The most viable set of objectives are those which are mutually determined by managers and staff, teachers, and students, and the appropriate peers. Moreover, the mutually determined objectives of the respective employees should be an outgrowth of the goals of the institution. In this respect, the approach by objectives can and should be the guiding light for the system which subscribes to it. As a matter of illustration, consider a hypothetical community college with a continuing education office of three managers and two hundred faculty.

Suppose that the managers plan and operate their continuing education responsibilities on a management-by-objectives system. If community demand indicated the need for more classes to be held *off-campus,* the manager responsible for these extension classes would have as one of his objectives for that year to establish more extension locations by the beginning of the fall semester. The manager might judge the achievement of this objective by stating that it would be considered accomplished when at least ten extension locations are in operation by the first day of classes in the fall. Other items that are typically found in the manager's list of objectives might be the number of new courses, seminars, or workshops to be offered; an average class size of eighteen students; an average instructor's salary of $15 per teaching hour.

At the same time the managers of the continuing education program are pursuing their objectives, members of the faculty would be planning or teaching their courses by the objective approach. A typical example of an objective from a continuing education course in "Air Line Ticketing and Reservations" might be:

> By the end of the second class, the student will be able to locate the times and carriers for a given day.
> This objective will be considered achieved when the student can locate all of the alternative times and carriers for a given trip within two minutes from the domestic airlines guide.

Objectives that begin with such terms as "to appreciate," "to understand," and "to learn" are taboo because they are not measurable. And if an objective cannot be measured, it can never be determined if that objective has been achieved. While the foregoing is the essence of the objectives approach, a more desirable and comprehensive program that is planned by objectives might also include supportive materials or measuring instruments for specific objectives.

Proper development and utilization of the objectives approach provides:

1. A written (as opposed to verbal) directional guide for activity.
2. An efficient means for evaluating a program, course, or person for achievement, progress, control, or reward (merit raises).
3. A reference tool for selecting appropriate materials, content, methods, or budgeting allocations.
4. A bridge to the communications gap by clearly setting forth student-teacher and line-staff expectations.
5. An informational source for the demands of accountability.

6. A flexible system which can adjust to innovational changes.

In spite of these attributes, the objectives approach does not hold all of the answers. It presents some very real concerns that must be dealt with if it is to be a success. For example, extensive planning is at the very core of this approach, and extensive planning takes time. Time is a precious item in the eyes of most people today and the adjustment thereof usually requires compensation in the form of more money or reduced work load. And whenever institutional or individual pocketbooks are under review, a reexamination of budgets and, hence, philosophies, is usually not far off. Meanwhile, the persons involved must consider their willingness to reorient professional attitudes to a more systematic approach to education. Further, they must be willing to accept the additional planning time that is required in the conversion from their present instructional methods.

Without a doubt, there are those who are hesitant to change their administrative or teaching ways to the behavioral-objectives approach. By way of fable, Robert Mager in *Preparing Instructional Objectives* suggests that the hesitation of these people might be their downfall.

Fable

Once upon a time a Sea Horse gathered up his seven pieces of eight and cantered out to find his fortune. Before he had traveled very far he met with Eel, who said, "Psst. Hey, bud. Where 'ya goin'?"

"I'm going out to find my fortune," replied the Sea Horse, proudly.

"You're in luck," said the Eel. "For four pieces-of-eight you can have this speedy flipper, and then you'll be able to get there a lot faster."

"Gee, that's swell," said the Sea Horse, and paid the money and put on the flipper and slithered off at twice the speed. Soon he came upon a Sponge, who said, "Psst. Hey, bud. Where 'ya goin'?"

"I'm going out to find my fortune," replied the Sea Horse.

"You're in luck," said the Sponge. "For a small fee I will let you have this jet-propelled scooter so that you will be able to travel a lot faster."

So the Sea Horse bought the scooter with his remaining money and went zooming through the sea five times as fast. Soon he came upon a Shark, who said, "Psst. Hey, bud. Where 'ya goin'?"

"I'm going out to find my fortune," replied the Sea Horse.

"You're in luck. If you'll take this short cut," said the Shark, pointing to his open mouth, "you'll save yourself a lot of time."

"Gee, thanks," said the Sea Horse, and zoomed off into the interior of the Shark, there to be devoured.

The moral of this fable is that if you're not sure where you're going, you're liable to end up someplace else—and not even know it.

The moral of this fable also illustrates the importance of planning and its impact upon performance. As we have seen in this chapter so far, these principles can be equally applicable to instruction and management in education as a whole and to continuing education in particular. Continuing education would do well to be especially alert to these features in all their forms. Management by Objectives (MBO), for example, is another variation of this concept that has gained growing attention in recent years.

Management by Objectives (MBO)

MBO is primarily a business/industrial concept. As such, it first came to light for popular consumption when Peter Drucker wrote *The Practice of Management* in 1954.[1] Based upon years of experience as a student of and participant in the business/industrial sector, Drucker recorded in this book some of the more effective management practices that he had observed. One or the more important observations was that the most efficient organizations tended to be characterized by a high degree of planning and forethought. Drucker explained that because of their emphasis upon planning, these organizations usually experienced a greater degree of success in achieving their corporate goals than others. In other words, the companies that knew where they were going had a better chance of getting there.

While Drucker was obviously referring to a goal-directed system of management, it is doubtful that he alone can be attributed with the founding of MBO. The whole behaviorist movement, as well as an arrival of an increased emphasis upon accountability—the ability to explain, defend, or justify positions and actions—were factors that probably had an untold influence upon Drucker and other objectives-oriented persons such as Robert S. McNamara. During his tenure in the president's cabinet, McNamara earned quite a reputation for implementing a performance-based management system throughout the Department of Defense. Wherever an account of the development of PPBS (Planning Programming Budgeting System) is made, there is usually some reference made to the Defense Department's operation during the McNamara years.

Somewhere near the end of the McNamara years, the success and notoriety of performance-based operations began to have a noticeable effect in educational quarters. It was just about this time that Robert Mager's classical book, *Preparing Instructional Objectives*,[2] appeared on the scene and advised educators that learning could be and should be measured. All the while that educators were reviewing their timeworn pedagogy in terms of behavioral objectives, some selected business firms were retooling their operations along the same lines. One of the leading spokesmen that emerged from the industrial movement was George Odiorne.[3]

Some of the better known companies that have switched to a Management-by-Objectives system are General Mills, General Motors, General Electric, Honeywell, IBM, and Regis Paper. Still under the influence of instruction by objectives à la Mager and soaking up the glowing report of Management by Objectives à la George Odiorne et al., a growing number of educational institutions began to implement MBO. The University of Tennessee, the University of Utah, and William Rainey Harper College are but a few of the schools where MBO success stories prevail.

The System

As is usually the case with academia, there are about as many definitions of MBO as there are authorities. So to keep the reader from being inundated with a wealth of footnotes, here is one definition: MBO is a systematic and continual process whereby the members of a given management team pursue mutually agreed upon goals of and for their organization. Enroute to completing this process, MBO typically proceeds through the following steps:

1. Institutional goals are established.
2. Individual (managerial) goals are set and pursued.
3. Performance reviews are held periodically to evaluate progress in achieving goals.
4. Appraisal sessions are held at the end of the year to assess and reward accomplishment.

In step number one, managers throughout the institution submit their suggestions for institutional goals to their superiors sometimes prior to the beginning of the managerial year. Because of the inherent relationship between management and money, it is recommended that the goals be submitted in synchronization with the preparation of the budget so that the corporate goals of the institution are in tune with the resources available for their attainment. This is especially true if the organization subscribes to a PPBS format.

The goals are then reviewed and refined as they filter through the varying levels of the managerial hierarchy to the top of the organization. They are checked for continuity and compatibility with the current economic and social climate the mission statement of the institution, past and present long range plans for the organization, and the job descriptions of the respective managers. Once the goals for the institution have been formulated, they are distributed to each manager in the organization.

In this second step of the MBO process, managers are charged with the responsibility of developing the performance goals for their respective offices that reflect the overall direction of the institution as indicated by the institutional goals. In writing performance objectives, the manager consults frequently with his superiors, subordinates, and counterparts to insure that everybody will be working in harmony, and most important of all, towards the same end. Starting with the next year then, the manager will begin to work towards achieving his objectives.

As the year proceeds, the manager will periodically (three or four times) meet with his superior to review the progress made in achieving his goals. These performance-review sessions provide a good opportunity for the manager and his subordinate (or superior) to discuss areas for improvement of managerial skills. For this reason, these meetings can often be called Coaching and Development as well as Performance Review Sessions. In addition to Coaching and Development, and Performance Review, these sessions also enable the management team to revise, add, or delete goals as the circumstances so warrant.

The final performance review session of the year and step number 4 of the MBO system is, for all practical purposes, an appraisal session. The purpose of this meeting is to assess the degree to which the manager has accomplished his goals for the year. Based upon the degree of accomplishment, a person may be rewarded accordingly for his performance with a salary increase or promotion or whatever.

The Mechanics

There are varying styles of writing management objectives. Whatever the style, the basic content is the same. The desired result is stated in terms of how and to what degree it is going to be achieved. Stating the criteria for successful accomplishment in ranges rather than in fixed amounts introduces an element of flexibility into a managerial system which is sometimes criticized for its rigidity. Today the more popular styles for writing objectives are the simple sentence, the qualifying paragraph, and the columnar grid, as follows.

Simple Sentence: My objective is to increase the average class size to twenty-five or thirty students per section for the 1976–77 academic year.

Qualifying Paragraph: My objective is to maximize classroom-building utilization. This objective will be considered achieved when:

1. An analysis of past, present, and projected building utilization is made by February 1, 1977.

2. 90–100% of the scheduled classes actually take place.

3. One-half of the classes are scheduled in the morning and the remaining half in the afternoon.

The Columnar Grid:

The Result Area	The Activity	Criteria
Staff Utilization	Increase efficient use	1. 95% of the faculty are teaching a full load by March 18, 1977.
		2. Released time option will be phased out by June 1, 1977.

Upon being written, managerial goals can be placed in any one of four categories: routine, problem, innovative, and personal. Routine goals are those which are an everyday aspect of the job such as preparing the budget, developing publicity, or staffing positions. Problem goals are an attempt to resolve an existing dilemma. Innovative goals are those which are new to the management of a given operation. They have never been tried before. Personal goals are personal objectives which a manager sees as being relevant to his position. In the case of educators, this might take the form of joining professional organizations, publishing, or working on an advanced degree.

Management experts are pretty well in agreement that the higher the managerial position that a person occupies, the less time he should spend on routine goals and the more time on innovative goals. Correspondingly, lower echelon managers should have a greater proportion of their time spent in routine goals and less on innovative.

The Good and the Bad

MBO cannot solve all of an organization's problems. It is merely one more tool that a manager can draw upon in meeting the responsibilities and obligations of his position. If an organization plans to implement MBO, it should not be misled into thinking that it is an entirely rosy proposition. MBO often requires some rethinking of current management practices. This rethinking may reveal the need for an in-service administrative development program to equip managers with the skills to successfully implement an MBO system. Because the manager becomes more accountable and skillful, the entire administrative structure might need reorganization to reflect a decentralized decision-making process.

MBO is a new concept to most managers and as such it can generate an atmosphere of apprehension. This apprehension is probably dealt with best by phasing into MBO over a period of two to five years. In fact, most authorities agree that it takes MBO that long to reach optimal maturity. Given these eventualities, MBO could prove to be expensive. And to top it all off, the transition is not easy. It requires a lot of hard work for all parties concerned. The growing number of organizations that are switching to MBO, however, indicates that the effort might be well worth the reward.[4] One of the potential rewards is a more accountable management system.

In this day of accountability, organizations must demonstrate accomplishment. Enroute to demonstrating accomplishment, organizations are finding that it pays to place more and more attention to the planning function. And because planning is the backbone of MBO, Management by Objectives serves to meet a very real need. In addition to accomplishment, planning also yields economies.

MBO is often championed for its ability to get the most and the best from its practitioners. And because it promotes quality and productivity, the organization tends to get more for its dollar. In addition to stretching the dollar, MBO also deals with the problem of communication. If the appraisal and performance review are properly conducted, they can provide an effective vehicle for colleagues to exchange their professionally relevant needs and wants. All in all, these positive features tend to breed high morale and even more.

There simply isn't enough space here to tell the whole story of MBO and the role it can take in continuing education management. Just as it would be similarly impossible to cover all of the influences of appropriate continuing education facilities and their impact on instruction. But it is to be hoped that this brief sojourn into both areas will have been sufficient enough to demonstrate this aspect of continuing education.

Building for Continuing Education

In a very real sense, continuing education is an orphan. Not unlike Gulliver's dilemma, it is usually a program without a home. Except in a few leading colleges and universities and corporate giants, the continuing education program is a tenant or must share the facilities of a parent or other organization. Rarely, if ever, do continuing education programs occupy facilities solely built for and used by their clientele.

Many of the problems that arise when continuing education must utilize facilities designed for other purposes are evident. Some institutions, such as public and private schools, bus children right to the front door. Therefore, these sites rarely accommodate the older person who rides the city buses or drives his own car. Proximity to public transportation and ample parking space for private autos are often not available to the mature learner who enrolls for a course at a public or private school facility.

Although the architectural trend appears to be changing,

public schools and some civic buildings are often gloriously set off by numerous and sometimes steeply inclined steps. The typical adult is not as spry or physically capable as his younger brethren. Ramp approaches are much more conducive than steps to a pair of middle-age legs that have labored all day. Ramps are also more appropriate for the person with a disability, a problem that does not often plague children. For these same reasons and because some people are often hesitant about returning to school, the continuing education segments of a shared facility should be distinct from other parts of the buildings and should be close to the main entrance. Adherence to these suggestions will demand a minimum of physical and mental exertion from the less physically able. Any reservations a person has about getting involved in continuing education should not be bolstered by the frustrations of wandering through a whole building in order to find his class, meeting, or registration area. Continuing education facilities should have conference and seminar rooms of varying size and flexible arrangement with built-in audiovisual fixtures. The autonomy and maturity that people bring to the situation demands more accommodation than the stiff-backed wooden desks of a schoolroom. An effective climate for learning is enhanced by a relaxed and comfortable atmosphere, where participation is not hindered by physical arrangements. Such an atmosphere is not rendered by rows of desks rigidly set to receive the lesson. Nor is this atmosphere established when the conference and seminar rooms are disturbed by the clanking stubbornness of a projector screen being set up or the maze of extension cords necessary to reach the only outlet in the room. Likewise, the setting sun peering through the closed venetian blinds upon the screen of a TV set that has lost all of its composure while being moved from one room to another hardly enhances the climate for learning. Accordingly, each conference and seminar room, as well as any appropriate area in the facility, should be outfitted with as many audiovisual aids and accessories as the budget will allow.

A facility designed solely for continuing education

should be a one-level structure. Where facilities are shared and subject to disturbances to the conference and seminar rooms, the programs should be housed in a separate segment of the facility. To further minimize disturbances, all rooms should be windowless and soundproof to avoid distracting vistas and noises. The fact that many continuing education activities are held at night demands that all rooms be equipped with superior lighting. Where the climate demands, air conditioning is an essential feature of an effective learning climate.

To serve the person who comes to class directly from his place of employment or vice versa, a snack bar or cafeteria should be provided. A gnawing stomach hardly improves the concentration of the participant. To relieve the discomfort of smoke-filled rooms and corridors, extra ventilation should be installed.

The focal point of the entire structure should be the library or its more recent adjunct, the materials resource center. It should be centrally located, invitingly adorned and adequately stocked. Where resources permit, overnight living quarters would be a desirable amenity. Such a facility would serve out-of-town guests to the program as well as providing living quarters for participants in accelerated workshops and institutions.

The above stated needs are the opinions of studies and authorities as revealed in the literature. In order to test the validity of some of these opinions, they were arranged, as representative as possible, in questionnaire form. The questionnaire was sent and responded to by a panel of ten experts and a class of thirty-two graduate students in continuing education. The panel of experts were sent a list of twenty-six architectural requirements for a continuing education facility. The respondents were asked to indicate the degree of importance they attached to each of the requirements. Each requirement had five possible ratings: *Of Great Importance; Very Important; Important; Of Some Importance; Of No Importance.* At the end of the questionnaire, the respondents were asked to indicate any suggestions, changes, deletions or additions that they thought were necessary to make this list more complete.

The panel of experts and the continuing education students agreed on many of the architectural requirements. They both felt that the following items were *Very Important*:

1. Accessibility of site to public and private transportation.
2. Conference and seminar rooms of varying size and flexible arrangement.
3. An abundance of audiovisual capabilities and equipment.
4. Activity areas separated from study areas.
5. A multi-purpose, auditorium-like room for meetings, dances, concerts, and plays.

Both groups gave an average rating of *Important* to the following architectural requirements:

1. Level or near-level building approaches; where necessary, ramps instead of steps.
2. Most facilities within two-hundred yards of the main entrance.
3. Windowless and soundproof rooms.
4. Bilateral lighting with a minimum of forty-five-foot-candle power.
5. Rooms and/or areas for displays and exhibits.
6. Recreation areas and lounges.
7. Optimum air conditioning capabilities (includes temperature-control as well as proper air ventilation and circulation).
8. Distinct segments of the building for older students when facilities are shared.

Neither group felt that the need for a cafeteria was more than of *Some Importance*. In spite of unanimity on these points, the panel of experts and the students disagreed on many of the architectural requirements.

The panel of experts rated the following items as *Very Important:*

1. Approximately one hundred twenty square feet of public parking space per projected student utilization of facilities.

2. Ample storage space for student projects and teacher materials.

The students rated these same items as *Important.*

Conversely, the students rated: Office space reserved exclusively for registration, counseling, information and administration, and a centrally located materials resource center as *Very Important,* while the panel rated these same items as *Important.*

The students felt that the following items were *Important*:
1. Upper story occupancy should be prohibited except by elevator or escalator;
2. It would be desirable to have at least three multipurpose workrooms and three multipurpose laboratories;
3. Study carrels should be available;
4. A first-aid room should be on the site.

The panel of experts, however, felt that these items were only *Of Some Importance.*

Conversely, the panel of experts indicated that snack bars and overnight living quarters for guests and out-of-town participants were *Important.* The students, however, indicated that these items were only *Of Some Importance.*

An analysis of the suggestions that were added to the end of the questionnaire by the respondents could be summarized into two broad headings. First, it was advised that it was impossible and inaccurate to formulate the architectural criteria for a continuing education facility that would or could apply to all program possibilities and demands. The suggestion continued that the architectural requirements for a continuing education facility must be determined by a given facility. The clientele, the community, and the program are all determinants that could ostensibly vary the architectural requirements of a continuing education facility.

A second suggestion was that the questionnaire should include items concerning adult-sized furniture, equipment, and facilities. It was further recommended that it should include items referring to audiovisual aids, secretaries, and other desirable amenities within the working budget. These suggestions implied that any future analysis of the architectural requirements of a continuing education facility should encompass all of the environmental systems which come into play in the total educational design.

In order for an architect to transpose the aforementioned comments and findings into an architectural design, it is necessary that they be put in the form of EDSPECS (educational specifications). Sheets and Hostetler[5] tell us that:

EDSPECS are:
1. Based on the philosophy of the institution.
2. Based on the educational program to be offered.
3. Developed around function (tasks) to be performed.
4. An exact description, in writing, of spaces required and the activities to take place in them, including identifiable interaction between spaces.
5. Instructions to the master planner or the architect.

EDSPECS are not:
1. Line drawings of space desired (circle diagrams may be used to show space relationships).
2. Exact square-footage instructions to the architect (square footages are best used where feasible as suggested minimums per student station, approximations, or illustrations of space size).
3. Thought of in terms of building (e.g., science building, cafeteria, administration building, etc.)
4. To design a campus or a facility—that is the architect's job. EDSPECS simply state what is to go on there.

Combining this prescription for EDSPECS with the information available for a given proposed continuing education facility might result in the following model:

Educational Specifications for Building "R"

I. *Philosophy and Objectives*
The function of Building R should be to provide the facilities and environment necessary to promote the

type of learning activities that are most conducive to a student who has ceased to have a full-time commitment to formal education and has, in turn, elected to pursue learning-delivery systems that better complement his existing life-style en route to self-fulfillment.

II. *Curriculum*

The curriculum housed in the building will consist of short courses (one to twelve weeks), seminars and workshops (one to five days), lectures, and cultural events. The content of this curriculum shall be distributed according to the following categories that are currently prescribed by the state or local educational board:

A. Homemaking
B. Improving Family Circumstances
C. Personal Development
D. Development and Review of Vocational Skills
E. Intellectual and Cultural Studies
F. Health, Safety, and Environment
G. Community and Civic Development
H. Developmental and Preparatory Studies/Skills

III. *Teaching-Learning Activities*

Building R should have the capability of making available the latest in instructional media. Although the student/teacher exchange will be a mainstay of this learning environment, it will also be heavily weighted with alternative styles such as individualized instruction, audiovisual media and independent study.

IV. *Facilities Specifications*

The continuing education center should:

A. Effectively meet 80 percent of the total short courses in conference demands placed upon it in terms of instruction, dining, living, and parking needs. The remaining 20 percent of needs could be met by regular facilities.
B. Approximate the following area assignments:

Item	Number	Capacity	Approximate Square Feet
Auditorium	1	300	9,000
Large lecture room	1	100	3,000
Large seminar rooms (carpet, tables)	5	300	10,000
Multipurpose classrooms (Desk, armchairs)	10	500	16,000
Multipurpose laboratory	1	50	2,000
Banquet room	1	400	6,000
Medium banquet room	1	150	2,500
Small banquet room	1	50	1,000
Kitchens	1	—	1,000
Offices (including secretary)	10	—	2,000
Supply room	1	—	200
Utility room	1	—	200
Day-care room and area	1	100	2,000
Registration desk and area	1	—	100
Maintenance and supply room	1	—	200
Light work and storage area	1	—	500
Lobbies	2	—	400
Snack and lounge area	1	—	500
Display and exhibit area	1	—	Hallways
Audiovisual room	1	—	300
Checkroom	1	—	200
First aid room	1	—	100
One-bedroom units	5	5	2,000
Two-bedroom units	20	40	7,000
Totals	70	1,995	66,200

C. Have sufficient parking space to accommodate three hundred cars.

D. Have highest priority given to the construction of instructional and dining facilities with living accommodations appearing in subsequent building phases.

E. Have about ten to fifteen acres for the center and its surroundings.

F. Pay attention to the aesthetic quality such as landscaping, view, decor, and the avoidance of a hotel-like atmosphere.

G. Pay attention to the relationship of the interior and exterior areas. For example, the conference and instructional facilities should be discernibly separate from the residential aspects of the facility.

H. Stress acoustics, lighting, ventilation, and other physical adaptations for the mature person, i.e., ramps instead of stairs, escalators and elevators, close to parking, and so on.

I. Be close to outside recreational opportunities and the rest of the resources of the campus.

J. Have all of the physical complements necessary to offer maximum utilization of modern and future audiovisual equipment, etc.

K. Be conceived of as a facility where the participants in courses and seminars can work, sleep, study, eat, and relax together within the same physical plant while still remaining within commutable distance of the heart of the regular college campus with all of its resources available to the continuing education center.

L. Have an administrative center to the front and center of the physical facility.

Conclusion

This paper is by no means intended to be the final word in developing a continuing education facility. As the reader will readily note, its comments stop abruptly short of the construction phase, a subject of its own and of greater scope than this article would permit. Rather, the major purpose has been to draw attention to the need for the development of specialized learning facilities for continuing education, be they alterations to existing structures designed for other clientele or an entirely new facility designed specifically for continuing education. It is to be hoped that this and similar efforts will combine with other resources to promote the concept of a distinct continuing education facility.

3 The Continuing Education Curriculum

The excitement and potential of continuing education lies in its base of innovation and spontaneity. Relatively unshackled by tradition, it is usually free to pursue whatever tack appears best to meet the myriad needs of its varied clientele—be it staff development for government and industry; life enrichment for given community groups, i.e., women; literacy education for minorities; or special programming for the church or the medical profession.

By way of recounting specific curriculum examples from continuing education programs, the purpose of this chapter is to illustrate the potential and breadth of the continuing education curriculum. The message of the chapter is that the continuing education curriculum and the community needs are one. The reader is challenged to analyze his community's needs and devise a tentative continuing education curriculum accordingly. In so doing, attention should be taken to consider and specify the methods and means of needs assessment, funding, staffing, facilities, and program evaluation, with especial notice given to an analysis of community leadership patterns.

Developing Community Leadership

Community leaders, community needs, and community colleges need to get together more often. The following account is a report on one such integrated effort. At most, its data elements and program model can serve as a valuable reference point for similar endeavors. At least, it could be the catalyst for added impetus in developing community leadership.

Introduction

Developing the leadership potential of a given community into a viable and effective action force is an oft slighted and sorely needed goal of continuing education. The bulk of the problem lies in identifying the needs of prospective leaders in a given community and developing programs that meet these needs. One such effort was recently conducted by a suburban community college caught up in the dynamism of instant cities, homes, shopping centers, apartments, clubs, organizations, and governments.

In an effort to provide substance and promise to the emerging leadership of the community, the William Rainey Harper College, Palatine, Illinois gathered the advice and counsel of selected representatives of the ruling order (mayors, city managers, club presidents, newspaper editors) via an advisory committee. Based on the committee's recommendations, the idea of a community leadership center was conceived and transmitted to a state agency for its reaction and possible funding. A $10,000-grant was soon forthcoming and the development wheels went into action.

Sample Characteristics

In an attempt to measure the community's leadership needs, 176 persons chosen at random from lists of community and civic agencies and holding elected (75 percent) or appointed (25 percent) positions in their respective organizations were surveyed regarding the leadership center idea.

The 176 respondents indicated that they were active (held a title or served on a committee) in 294 different organizations. This finding suggested that the typical community leader was probably a leader in two or more organizations at one time and that the total leadership of the com-

Figure 3–1
Method of Leadership Selection

Selection Method	Number	Percent
Elected	132	75
Appointed	44	25
Total	176	100

munity was apparently in the hands of a relatively few (the population of the college district was over 250,000) people. Equally as interesting and certainly grounds for future studies was the obvious fact that the masses were not actively involved in the direction of their community. Verification of this observation was evidenced in later questions where the responses indicated that one of the greatest needs of community and civic organizations was human resources. Stated in other terms, the average club or organization could get a lot more done if it only had the help (people involvement).

Further study was also suggested by the response that more than twice as many men as women held leadership roles in the community.

Figure 3–2
Leadership Distribution By Sex

Sex	Number	Percent
Female	55	31
Male	121	69
Total	176	100

While there are many good explanations for this finding, it certainly went a long way in dispelling any myths that the community was run by well-to-do, social-climbing fems and do-gooding little old ladies. Admittedly, the preponderance of political units surveyed and their preponderantly male staffing patterns (be that wrong or right, good or bad) certainly biased this finding. Nevertheless, it does suggest that the majority of leadership positions in this community were occupied by men.

The age distribution represented a fairly normal curve

with the greatest amount of leadership involvement between the ages of thirty and forty-nine. This could mean that these were the ages when leadership-prone adults experienced the opportunity to share the time of their greatest personal, family, and career responsibilities with their community. For the homemaker, the children may have grown to school age or were old enough to tag along, care for themselves, or be supervised by others. For the career person, vocational mobility may have become solidified and relocation less of a probability.

Figure 3–3
Age Distribution
(N=176)

Age	Number	Percent
Under 20	0	0
20–29	19	11
30–39	54	31
40–49	56	32
50–59	31	18
60–69	13	7
70 and over	3	1
Totals	176	100

It was discouraging to note that the twenty–twenty-nine age bracket showed such meager representation. Perhaps, it was because their personal, family, and career responsibilities had not freed them for leadership participation as yet. It is to be hoped that it was not a rejection of the system in the wake of Watergate.

Interestingly, 26 percent of the "leaders" were over the age of fifty. This appears to be in keeping with some of the projections that tell us that our population as a whole is and will be getting older. It was comforting to learn that older Americans were already beginning to lend present and future generations the benefit of their knowledge and experience in a leadership capacity. We hope that this is the first sign of an ever growing trend. In all honesty, however, the skewness toward the older end of the curve probably also suggested that elected and appointed leaders were chosen for their experience and maturity and that only the most qualified adults tended to exhibit this at a younger age.

The zero leadership participation of persons under twenty was a bias of the study. All of the organizations surveyed were what could be considered adult-oriented. While the under-twenty leadership participation would probably even be low in a more accurate study, it would, more than likely, be wrong to say that this age group did not participate at all in the leadership of the community, i.e., Young Republicans and Young Democrats.

The data regarding educational preparation of leaders clearly suggested that the community leaders tended to be the better educated persons in the community.

Figure 3–4
Educational Preparation

	Percent
Some high school	1
High school graduate	6
Some college	12
College degree	32
Some graduate work	11
Graduate degree	38
	100

Ninety-three percent had had some college; 32 percent held a bachelor's degree and 38 percent held a graduate degree. Meanwhile, 7 percent had a high school education or less. These results were probably influenced by the extensive amount of college training typical of local government managers and by the calibre of the residents of this specific community. Nevertheless, it still suggested that it may be expected that education and leadership go hand in hand.

Needs Analysis

The proposed community leadership program gathered further justification when the respondents indicated that 73 percent had had no special in-service training for or orientation to their leadership positions.

Figure 3–5
Leadership Preparation

	Number	Percent
No special training	128	73
Some special training	48	27
Total	176	100

So, while the typical community leader was well educated, he or she was not necessarily prepared for his or her leadership role.

At this point in the study, the data indicated a need for leadership training for a well-educated, mature clientele. Responses to additional queries in the instrument helped to delineate the scope and nature of the probable response to this need.

For example, analysis of further data revealed that the concerns of the one hundred and seventy-six respondents were distributed as follows:

Figure 3–6
Organizational Concern

	Percent
Human resources (i.e., volunteer, bureau, senior citizen)	37
Land use (including zoning)	34
Education and training	23
Housing and facilities	23
Environment (including waste control)	21
Water management	15
Traffic management	14
Fund raising	9
Other	2
Total	100

The respondents further indicated that the resources they needed most in effectively pursuing the concerns and the goals of their organization were as follows:

Figure 3–7
Resources Needed

	Number of Respondents
Funding (dollars to implement mission)	123
Human resources (staff, clerks, citizen participation)	16
Time (to develop and promote)	16
Public relations (promotion and advertising)	10
Education and training (train staff, clerks and educate public)	9
Other (i.e., facilities)	2

Taking the Resources Needed with a projected educational program, it was not surprising to find that 20 percent of the total membership of the respective organizations (N = 3025) would partake in programs on financing projects (303) and motivating citizens (303).

Ostensibly both programs would be a step in the right direction toward solving the money and personnel concerns of community leaders.

Although it had not surfaced in earlier responses on the instrument, planning (454) emerged as the topic that would probably draw the largest number of attendees in a leadership program. Interagency cooperation was another subject that had not appeared in earlier queries. As the fourth most requested program, it suggested that a lot (272) of the leaders were looking to interagency cooperation for possible assistance in successfully pursuing the concerns and goals of their respective organizations.

Figure 3–8
Projected Participation Rate
N = 3025

Program	Number	Percent
Planning	454	15
Financing projects	303	10
Motivating citizens	303	10
Interagency cooperation	272	9
Public relations	242	8
Conducting meetings	212	7
Managing local government	212	7
Youth programs	151	5
Organizational design	121	4
Education and training	103	3
Solid waste	99	3
Library services	92	3
Parks and recreation	89	3
Health	73	2
Communications	68	2
Senior citizens	68	2
Land use and zoning	56	2
Recycling	54	1
Record keeping	39	1
Other	14	3
Total	3025	100

The remainder of the responses to the question regarding program interest was much as expected except for the items on education and training, land use and zoning, and housing and facilities. All of these items appeared earlier as predominant concerns of the respondents. Yet, all of them occupied relatively lesser roles when suggested as possible seminar topics. One interpretation of this could be that the community leadership felt that the emphasis of their leadership education should be more on the mechanics of building an effective organization and less on the substance of their respective concerns. In evidence hereto, attention should be drawn to the top half of the list of suggested topics. It dealt with elements of an organizational system whereas the lower half of the list dealt with subjects that represent the concerns of various organizations as typified in Figure 3–6.

Program Development

These findings were interfaced with the reactions and input of the leadership advisory committee and the observations of a community development consultant. The product of this interchange was the development of a series of leadership seminars.

Figure 3–9
Leadership Seminars

Boards	Staff	Citizens
Sept. 25 Open Forum: An Invitation to Community Action		
Oct. 9 Communications and small group dynamics	Oct. 23 Public relations	Oct. 3 How to become a participating citizen. How to get involved.
Nov. 13 Medium and long-range planning	Nov. 6 Zoning and land use	Nov. 21 The structure of local government
Dec. 11 How to analyze finances	Dec. 4 Where should the control be	Dec. 19 How to implement plans
Jan. 22 How to lead to a decision	Jan. 15 Grantmanship	Jan. 30 How to run an effective meeting
Feb. 5 How to analyze statutes and ordinances	Feb. 5 Waste disposal	Feb. 20 How to prepare a proposal
Mar. 5 Intergovernmental cooperation	Mar. 5 Intergovernmental cooperative	Mar. 20 Legislative monitoring
Apr. 2 Computer basics	Apr. 2 Computer basics	Apr. 17 Intergroup liaison

For several months preceding the program, a part-time salaried coordinator of the leadership program was to promote the curriculum to as many community organizations and political units as possible. In an effort to appeal to aspiring community leaders waiting in the wings, communitywide promotion was also sought through news releases, mailers, and so on. The program was to be initiated with a verbal invitation to community action and citizen participation from a well-known community leader of statewide or national stature. Within ten days of his or her address, the leadership seminar series would begin.

The curriculum was divided among three groups: governing board members, organizational staff members, and citizen participants. The curricular tracts did not, however, bar a member of one category from enrolling in a seminar of another category if he or she felt that to be of benefit. In fact, this kind of personal judgement was encouraged and provided for in one or two sessions where seminars were cross-listed between two categories.

The Leadership Advisory Committee advised that evenings would most likely attract the greatest number of students. The committee further designated the nights of the week that community organization meetings were least likely to conflict with the leadership seminars. The committee also advised that a $10.00 per person, per seminar fee would be in line with most organizational and personal budgets. Based on an expected average enrollment of twenty people per seminar, this monetary figure served as the revenue base for the self-supporting budget. The budget, in turn, was to support a part-time coordinator, a part-time secretary, publicity, supplies, travel and a corps of seminar leaders. The Advisory Committee and consultant advised that instructor fees could be kept at a minimum by intermingling the costlier outside experts with local resource persons, many of whom might teach at no cost or at a nominal one.

The program was to be held once a year, spanning two regular school semesters. Persons completing seven of nine seminars would receive a certificate of recognition. Each seminar would be evaluated by the participants and so too the entire program at the end of the year. Ongoing adjustments in the respective seminars and the program as a whole would be made accordingly.

The following year the program was implemented with marginal success. Inflationary fears and budgetary restrictions throughout the public sector measured the attraction of the seminars and workshops. Nevertheless, all was not for naught. Some valuable data had been gathered and the leadership potential and resources of the community had been clearly delineated. These contacts proved to be transposable throughout the curriculum of the continuing education program and extending it to many heretofore untouched sectors of the community, including the functionally illiterate and the racetrack set.

Continuing Education and Community Outreach

The influence of physiological limitations, psychological barriers, social phenomena, and educational relevance are recurring features in the literature of continuing education. Accompanying these prominent themes, the same literature usually goes on to discuss these influences as they have been dealt with in some sort of an institutional setting, i.e., in school, business, or church—the implication being that these places are the most appropriate places for continuing education instruction. Promising experiments have indicated, however, that continuing education instruction might be just as effective if it is taken out of the institutional setting and put into physical facilities that are more immediate, familiar, and relevant to the environment of the continuing education student.

Social scientists of all sorts have learned that taking the mountain (continuing education) to Mohammed (adult) is sometimes more effective, although not necessarily easier, than taking Mohammed to the mountain. For example, merely witness the social phenomenon of campaigning politicians, religious missionaries, and social workers. In each case, these professionals have repeatedly and apparently satisfactorily taken their program to the people. Where the objective is to contact, for one reason or another, a reluctant populace, community outreach has been a not too infrequent medium of communication. In addition to enhancing the possibility of establishing meaningful contact with a target group, community outreach can also assist the continuing educator in removing some of the physiological, psychological, and sociological barriers to the adult learning process.

After all, where limited physiological mobility might impair the adult's ability or desire to participate in a continuing education program at the local school, what better way to overcome that obstacle to the learning process than to conveniently offer the instruction right on his doorstep? If the adult is psychologically reluctant to jeopardize his social position or psychological self-esteem by having to return to a school building or other environment that tends to embarrass or belittle him, then providing the same continuing education opportunities in the familiar and therefore conducive atmosphere of his own culture is surely one tactic to be considered.

In mitigating the influence of physiological, psychological, and sociological influences upon the adult learner, efforts of community outreach can also provide a heretofore unknown degree of relevancy. It would be difficult for a continuing education program to be any more relevant than when it is available right in the midst of a given subculture and all of its unique traits.

While a good community outreach program can, in many respects, surmount a good number of the hurdles in continuing education, it will not resolve all of the problems of continuing education. In fact, it generates its own set of problems. The decision to take the program to the community necessarily means additional planning and coordinating on the part of the faculty and administrators. They must be willing and able to spend long hours in the arrangements for facilities and on the accompanying logistics of materials and supplies. Moreover, if the program is to remain an effective and viable instrument of continuing education, these efforts must be never ending.

A community outreach program also demands persevering professional commitment and extreme day-to-day flexibility on the part of all of the staff. Inconvenient travel to and from substandard learning environments must be taken in stride and never be permitted to detract from the overall continuing education mission. If facilities cannot be secured at nominal (or less) cost, then financial aspects of developing and offering a successful community outreach program will certainly present a heavy burden to be reckoned with.

After weighing the alternatives to, and the inherent problems of a community outreach program, one community college opted for this method of reaching the racetrack segment of its college community with continuing education instruction.

Racetrackers

Typical of their subculture, employees of racetracks—racetrackers—have their own set of social values, mores, and strata. Racetrackers are the product of the racetrack environment. By and large, these people follow the horses as they move from the closing date at one track to the opening date at another track. Racetrackers look to the parimutuel window for the big winner and their stepping-stone to a better tomorrow. They subsist from race to race on the meager sums they earn as sweat-walkers, exercise riders, stable boys, and in occasional odd jobs on and off the track.

Most, if not all, of their money goes back to the track in the form of parimutuel wagers, purchases from the track store, and rent for their substandard living units on the "back side." As might be expected, racetrackers are a motley combination of undereducated blacks, whites, and Chicanos. They are locked firmly on the lower rung of the pecking order by their betting habits, exploitive horse trainers, and their lack of education. And as might be expected, they rationalize their predicament by saying that the track is in their blood.

While the betting habit and exploitive horse trainers are not the immediate province of continuing education, their inhibiting influence can probably be lessened if the race-tracker can be equipped with the basic skills and knowledge that will enable him to qualify for other jobs and their corresponding life-styles. Based upon this premise and in conjunction with two local high school districts, the college took the initiative and arranged with the local racetrack authorities to offer continuing education instruction in the clubhouse two evenings per week for the 1972 racing season. And if it proved worthwhile, plans were in the offing to make arrangements with other racetracks and colleges to continue the program as one track closed and another opened.

The basic plan was to provide classes on the essentials of communication, reading, and mathematics, as well as a program preparatory to earning the High School Equivalency Certificate. The program planners realized, however, that it might take more than just the promise of being able to learn to read and write or to earn the equivalent of a high school diploma to attract the racetrackers. Therefore, the program was supplemented with courses that provided opportunities for other forms of self-discovery like creative art and Black history. In order to best serve the needs of the Mexican-American students, Spanish-speaking instructors were available. And in an attempt to make sure that the program was communicated to the racetracker, a full page ad was taken out in the track newspaper and written in a jargon that was not foreign to their field of experience.

At the first session, attendance was disappointing, with fewer than thirty students present. With each succeeding meeting, however, the enrollment grew, until more than a hundred people were attending classes. After a few weeks, the outlook for the program was nothing but optimistic. And when the racing season closed at this track, the educational program moved in total with the students to the next track. Whatever the outcome, the efforts expended hereto have not been in vain. If nothing else, they have demonstrated once again that continuing education and community outreach are compatible systems. Systems that can be extended equally as effective to women, business, religion, health and other segments of the program service area.

Women's Programs

At their founding, most community colleges take care to be aware of the problems confronting education today. This awareness soon becomes a continual process within the operation of the organization. In recent years, a more distinct observation of this process was that the female population had special family, work, and educational needs which were not being met. On the basis of this observation many community colleges have set about determining more closely the interests and expectations of the women in their community. The following model helps to illustrate how one community college dealt with this issue.

Determining Women's Needs

A need and interests survey of three thousand women was conducted to determine the subject, times, formats, and persons which appealed to them. It was evident from the analysis that various subgroups (i.e., age, interests, associations, and educational background) had widely different preferences. Because of this variance, an advisory committee was formed for women's programs to help bridge the gap between them. The Women's Advisory Board convened twice a month on an informal basis on the college campus.

Meanwhile, the college made an extra effort to open its facilities to all women's clubs and organizations within the community. Each time a women's club or organization took advantage of this invitation, a representative of the college was on the scene to elicit opinions and desires regarding women's programs, present and future. In addition to these endeavors, the college was forever receptive and exploitive of telephone inquiries, faculty-staff articulation with the community, and miscellaneous public contacts such as open house.

Figure 3–10

POST TIME FOR EDUCATION

ATENCION

JUNE 6 - AUGUST 15

Tuesday and Thursday—6:30 p.m.-9:00 p.m.
Quinella selections — Single Entry Selections
WIN — this opportunity.
PLACE — First Floor Clubhouse.
SHOW — up and be involved.

Pick a winner from the following favorites:

1ST RACE . . . 6:30 - 7:45

1. *English — as a second language.* Be able to talk to those about you at work and play (except the horses). The teacher is understanding of the problems of a non-English speaking person in this country.

2. *G.E.D. High School Diploma.* If you have not yet completed your *High School Education* and want to do so, this class will prepare you in the areas needed to pass the tests. A High School Equivalency Certificate is issued if you pass the G.E.D. tests.

3. *Basic Education.* Mathematics and Reading skills offered at the level you need. The work

Post Time para Educacion y Cultura
Junio 6 — Agosto 15
Martes y Jueves — 6:30 - 9:00 p.m.
Escoja uno o dos.
Gane — la oportunidad
Lugar — en el ipodramo
Presentese a estas clases valiosas
Escoja una ganadora de estas:

A. INGLES — SU SEGUNDO IDIOMA — 6:30 - 7:45

Poder hablar con personas alrededor de usted en el trabajo o donde sea. La maestra entiende los problemas de personas que no hablan ingles en este pais.

B. G.E.D. — 6:30 - 7:45

Si todavia noha terminado su educacion secundaria y la quiere terminar, estas clases le begins with your ability and ends at your ambition.

2ND RACE . . . 7:45 - 9:00

4. *Creative Art.* Use your hidden talent and create your own masterpieces. Basics of sketching, drawing, painting and color using pencil, charcoal and water colors.

5. *Black History.* Recognize and learn of the varied contributions of blacks in the History of the United States.

6. *Current Events.* Newspapers, books and outside resources used as basics for rap sessions. A wide variety of subjects talked about and explored.

HOW TO REGISTER

PLACE YOUR BETS (Sign Up) AT

PLACE: First Floor Clubhouse

TIME: 6:30 P.M. — Tuesday, June 6, 1972

English Second Language . . . Art

G.E.D. High School Certificate

Black History . . . Reading

Mathematics . . . Current Events

COST: $6.00 — Bet for one course selection.

$10.00 — Bet for two course selections.

---

pueden ayudar. Al pasar los examenes se les dara un certificado.

C. EDUCACIONES BASICAS

Lectura — 6:30 - 7:45
Matematicas — 7:45 - 9:00

Matematicas, y Lectura al nivel que usted necesita, se ofrecen tambien.

D. ARTE CREATIVO — 7:45 - 9:00

Use su talento ye haga una obra maestra. Se ensenaran lo basico de dibujos, pinturas y colores. Usaran lapizes, carboncillo y pinturas de agua.

E. HISTORIA DE NEGROS — 7:45 - 9:00

Contribuciones de los negros en la historia de los Estados Unidos.

F. SUCESAS DE ACTUALIDADES

Periodicos, libros, y recursos de afuera se usaran para charlar. Se discutiran una gran variedad de termas.

Registrese el primer dia de clases, el seis de junio.

Seis dolares ($6.00) por una clase.
Diez dolares ($10.00) por dos clases.

Needs, Interests, and Expectations

From these various sources, information was categorized, evaluated, and interpreted. Among the general topics for which the respondents showed the greatest preference were: 1. arts (including fine arts); 2. music; 3. fashion; 4. creative cooking; 5. social problems (crime, poverty, racism, drugs); 6. social sciences (foreign affairs, government, current events, psychology); 7. consumer problems; 8. environmental pollution; 9. public schools; 10. vocational training.

With regard to campus guests, the women indicated that Dr. Haim Ginott, Leonard Bernstein, and Paul Erlich were tops on their list. The women gave as reason for their preferences (needs), that in their primary role as homemakers, they were anxious to do the best job they could. Any type of educational experience that the college could offer that would afford them the opportunity to better their homemaking role would apparently be well received.

Many women had reached a stage in their lives when some of their responsibilities had lessened. Hence, they were seeking worthwhile endeavors to occupy their leisure time or companionship to replenish their narrowing circle of friends and relatives. Some women at this state of life sought to return to work. Usually, this meant learning an employable skill or refreshing one that had become rusty over the years. In many instances, it was safe (and not naive!) to assume that some women just wanted to learn for knowledge's sake. Admittedly, this was a rarity, but attempts were made to satisfy this and all other needs.

The Program

In order to meet some of these needs, interests, and expectations, several eight-week courses (one night a week for two hours) were offered. To wit: 1. Electronics for Women; 2. Secretarial Refresher Workshop; 3. Keypunch Operator; 4. Airline Career Preparation; 5. Medication Training for the Nurse; 6. Parent-Child Psychology; 7. Social Poise and Appearance; 8. Cooking on a Budget; 9. Fashion Workshop;

10. Textile Design; 11. Gourmet Cooking; 12. Foods of Other Lands; 13. Lingerie Construction; 14. Painting; 15. Ceramics; 16. Sculpture; 17. Calligraphy; 18. Human Motivation Seminar (for women).

Two programs that were designed as an outcome of this project and that were tremendously successful were a course concentrating on the role of women in our society and a short coeducational workshop on the husband-wife relationship. Hundreds of women participated in these original sessions and almost as many returned for class reunions months later. To the person, they had found solace and self-renewal in themselves.

The charges for all of these programs were minimal and intended only to meet costs. The average price for the typical eight-week course was $10. The fee for a one-day program, including luncheon, was also $10.

Success

Probably because of the extensive determination of needs, planning, and involvement, the program for women was a grand success. Participation patterns included women from all socioeconomic levels and interest groups. Eventually they became involved in the curriculum process of the whole college as well as the establishment of a day-care center for children of students. What had begun as the satisfaction of a community need became a cornerstone of the college processes.

Serving the Community Through Marketing and Management Seminars

Students of the community college movement are well aware that a major function of the comprehensive community college is to provide a well-rounded program of continuing educational, cultural, and recreational services to the community which it serves. An obvious and often influential interest within most college communities is that of business and industry. For the most part, the cultural and recreational needs of employees have remained the prerogative of the individual. The forward-looking business or industry, however, has taken education to heart and made it an ongoing program in the development of its staff and employees. Perhaps this concern and need of business and industry for a continuing program of education was best explained by Glenn Jensen in the March, 1971, issue of *Adult Leadership* entitled, "Peter, Paul, and Mary."

In the article, Jensen referred to the Peter principle as pronounced by Dr. Lawrence J. Peter of the University of Southern California. As the reader will recall, the Peter principle holds that "every employee in a hierarchy tends to rise to his level of incompetence." Dr. Jensen then reminded the reader that in June of 1970, Dr. Paul Armer of Stanford University came forth with the Paul principle. The Paul principle held that people reach a level of incompetence in the hierarchy because they fail to continue to learn. Dr. Armer proposed that sabbatical leaves be taken so that employees could refurbish their skills and educate themselves as to the latest developments in their given line of work.

Drawing upon the Peter and the Paul principles, Jensen offered the Mary principle, named after his wife. Essentially, the Mary principle is an extension of the Peter and Paul principles. The Mary principle holds that an employee will become obsolete and hence incompetent at his level of employment in the hierarchy in direct proportion to the extent that he fails to recognize or abandon traditional or out-of-date practices and ideas. Jensen cautions that the Mary principle might not sound as expressive as either the Peter or the Paul principles. Nevertheless, it should still have importance for continuing education because that is really what the entire business of continuing education is all about. By way of illustration, Jensen offers an analogy between the Mary principle and a Madison Avenue expression, "If it's working—it's likely out of date."

In effect, the marketing and management seminars offered by many colleges are a manifestation of the Peter, Paul, and Mary principles. These seminars provide businessmen with an opportunity to upgrade and refurbish skills (Paul principle) and/or to replace out-of-date practices with tomorrow's ideas (Mary principle). En route to manifesting the Paul and Mary principles, the workshops and seminars shed serious doubt upon the validity of the Peter principle. For if the members of any hierarchy continue to learn and professionally adjust to the changing times, they will remain competent and never reach a point in the orgaization that is beyond their ability. And as this occurs, the Peter principle will be relegated to nonsensical fiction.

Determining the Need for Seminars

A broad interpretation of the Peter, Paul, and Mary principles explains some of the reasons for serving the community with marketing and management seminars. This necessarily begs the question, however, as to how these and other specific conmunity needs are determined. Probably one of the most popularly used and occasionally reliable means of determining community needs is by a survey or a questionnaire. The value of a survey of the community at large or of the business interests in particular is usually overemphasized. Probably its greatest redeeming value lies in its potential for revealing general areas of interest and need. But in spite of this redeeming value, sole dependency on the survey method for needed information is discouraged. Attention must also be given to other means of securing accurate feedback of community needs.

One of these other means is trade publications. Often, successfully proven programs can be gleaned from professional journals and publications, including literature of continuing education programs at other schools and businesses. While this method of information smacks of program thievery, it should be recalled that educational ethics permit skullduggery under the guise of research.

Social trends are other indicators of the need for seminars. Who would deny that relevance, communication, ability, and accountability are current social trends that have found their way into the corporate minds and processes of educational and other social institutions during the last decade? To ignore the existence of these trends and to not consider their study (and others) through a seminar format would be an inexcusable mistake.

Polling the expectations of adult students who are currently enrolled in educational programs can serve as another accurate guide for directing programming efforts. After all, studies reveal that these people are the ones most likely to continue with the learning process. Offering seminars in keeping with their wants is not a surefire success; but it comes pretty close.

Limited success can also be experienced by playing professional hunches. Although it is not earmarked in the index or in the table of contents of continuing education textbooks, offering seminars on the impetus of whim has produced some surprisingly positive results. One must be prepared, however, to suffer the loss of time, effort and money (not to mention reputation and ego) that more often than not accompanies such a tactic.

Probably the best way of all to build a seminar responsive to needs is to involve representatives of the business community in the developmental process. By having the interested parties take an active role in planning the seminar, the program will be sure to meet the needs and expectations of a majority of the target population. By securing a broader participation in the planning process, the success of the seminar will be greatly enhanced and the need to recruit students will be lessened. Not only will the planners increase their firm's participation in the seminar but the seminar agenda will be more attractive to that given industry and other businessmen as a whole.

Planning the Program

Once the decision to hold a given seminar has been made, great pains should be taken to insure its success. For the outstanding success or the dismal failure of that seminar can hold untold consequences for future programs. It is a tough job to build a commendable program but it requires only minimal effort and time to earn a debilitating reputation.

In order to do a good job and to avoid the bad reputation, it might be wise to consider some of the following suggestions:

Students, Identify the target group at which the seminar will be aimed. Enlist the group's support in planning the program and in disseminating information about its availability. It is conceivable that a seminar might go unattended if it is not attractive to the group for which it was designed.

Subject Matter. Adults enter a learning experience with an expectation for immediate use of the knowledge they are to acquire. Hence, the subject matter of the seminars should be loaded with information and examples that are familiar to the students' environment. Moreover, the information in seminars should be practicable on the job in the near future and not a theoretical concoction that will expire from disuse before it is applied. If a seminar is not relevant and does not provide useful information, it will generate a wealth of negative word-of-mouth publicity that could bring discredit upon all future seminars as well as the one in question.

Cost. The cost of the program to the student should be kept as low as the budget will permit. Program developers must remember that there is a direct relationship between an adult desire to continue his education and the drain it will place on his billfold. While individual firms often pick up the educational tab of employees, this is not always the case. In some instances, the employee is reimbursed at a later date. Where this occurs, a high tuition charge might discourage enrollment in the seminar. So by keeping the costs low, a program director can hedge against this possibility. Programmers should also remember that public institutions can sometimes receive government or foundation funding to help cover program expenditures. Because of this funding, seminars can usually be offered for a lesser tuition rate than that which is charged by private firms which conduct similar programs.

Learning Atmosphere. Because the typical seminar participant is an adult, care should be taken to guarantee that the learning climate complements his particular psychophysiological makeup. This means that the furniture, lighting, acoustics, and temperature of the learning environment should be as conducive as possible to adult learning. This also means that the adult should feel free to ask questions without being embarrassed or without raising his hand. He should feel free to leave at any time during the seminar and for any reason. He should not be chastised for daydreaming or napping. All of this is not to say that the adult student should be coddled. But it is to say that his expectations as a learner should be dealt with in a mature manner. If his expectations are not being met by the seminar, then only incidental learning, if any at all, will occur.

Teachers. If a seminar leader can attract a multitude of students regardless of his topic and if an objective of the program is to attract the greatest number of students, then by all means use the "big names." A word of caution. Big names are expensive and they can play havoc with the budget. They can increase the cost of the seminar to a point where it discourages enrollment by the dollar-minded adult. Where the development of a comprehensive program of seminars is the major concern, however, teachers of varying reputation will probably have to be secured. Where this is the case, it is inportant that each seminar leader be reminded of the aforementioned principles of relevance and atmosphere.

Registration. The registration procedures for the seminar should be kept as simple and convenient as possible. Name, address, phone, firm, and money are really all that are needed. Pamphlets, fliers, brochures and other printed publicity can easily include a registration blank requesting these items.

Evaluation. Continued success or failure can hinge on this item. An ongoing system of seminar evaluation provides the feedback needed for the evaluation of seminar leaders and seminar content. A properly designed evaluation system can also provide insight for additional seminar topics.

Summary

In offering a comprehensive program of seminars and workshops to the community it should be recalled that corporate as well as individual needs are being served. A business is only as sound and competent as its employees. If they rise to a level of incompetence (Peter principle) because they have failed to upgrade their skills (Paul principle) or to change outdated practices (Mary principle) then the business in which they are employed will also reach a level of incompetence. When sales begin to lag and the competition begins to gain the upper hand, it may be that a given business has reached its level of incompetence. And in the last analysis, the preservation of free enterprise might well be the real reason for serving the community through marketing and management seminars, just as the preservation of Western spiritual concepts may be the symbolic motive for the continuing attempts of continuing education to become involved in religious programs.

Thank You, Mr. Rosenquist!

At first sight (and for several glimpses thereafter), Max Rosenquist wasn't what one might call an overly impressive person. His motley appearance hardly projected charisma. Moreover, he spoke with an evangelistic undertone that immediately raised the suspicion that his ulterior motive was to use some part of the college curriculum as a pulpit for his cause. But as is so often the case, looks can be deceiving and you can't always judge a book by its cover. And so it was with Max. His first impressions didn't bear out in the turn of events that followed. And luckily they didn't because as it turned out, Max Rosenquist was just what the doctor had ordered! But perhaps a little bit of an explanation is in order.

William Rainey Harper college had tried every possible approach to develop a viable continuing education program for the religious segment of the community. Articulation meetings were held with religious leaders and organizations to solicit their support and participation in planning a program of religious instruction. Guest speakers addressed women's church auxiliaries and civic organizations and revealed the wealth of untold services that the college could provide. Ministers, pastors, and priests were approached individually for their assistance in program planning and recruiting. Religious groups were invited to campus for private tours and luncheons. Special efforts were made to see that every piece of public relations mail that left the college fell into the hands of a religious entity. But the efforts were of no avail. Not one continuing education class, seminar, or workshop in religion ever enrolled enough students to be held.

Disappointing as this was, it could hardly be attributed to a narrow scope of offerings. Fron the very formal academic presentation to the informal discussion group, from "Philosophy of Religion" to "Religions of the World" to "Contemporary Religions: Values and Morals," the college experienced nothing but disinterest. Of course there was always the possibility that the need for a continuing education program on religion was being adequately met by the individual churches and other religious organizations. But verification of this suspicion with religious leaders in the community was not substantiated. Just when the college was about to give up on continuing education programs for the religious community, Rosenquist came along.

Max had been assigned to the college campus by his minister to provide whatever spiritual guidance and leadership he could to the student body. This idea wasn't really new. It had been tried on other campuses across the nation with varying degrees of success. In fact, this college had tried it the year before with a representative from another faith. But his I-am-going-to-be-like-one-of-the-students approach soon led to his quick demise. Because of this blatant and embarrassing failure, Max's way had not been paved.

Well aware of his predecessor's fate, Max took to his task undaunted. He scheduled meetings with what appeared to be the appropriate persons at the college. But after several conferences, many cups of coffee, and a bad case of "sitting pains," the luster of his missionary zeal began to dull. After being shuttled from the philosophy department to the student activities office, he finally came to rest outside of the continuing education door.

His introductory handshake seemed to take forever. Had one known of the frustrations and disappointments that Max had experienced to that point in the day, one could have easily surmised that Max was afraid to let go for fear that I might leave the room and never come back. And if he did, he would never get to explain his ideas regarding the spiritual scene on the college campus. After what seemed like an agonizing forever, the handshake ended and Max was invited to sit down and to speak his piece.

Max spoke of forming a nondenominational, coeducational organization dedicated to the purpose of providing a forum for persons who wanted answers about religion. In addition to informative discussions, "Seekers," as it was to be called, would also sponsor tours, guest speakers, and distribute educational religious literature. Max also suggested that it might be a good idea for a class or classes in, of, or about religion to be offered on the campus. At this point, he was reminded of all the continuing education efforts and failures in the area of religion and that it might be difficult to overcome this negative precedent.

Unaffected by this defeatist attitude, Max asked if the office of continuing education would assist him in arranging for some sort of religious class to be held on the college campus. If for no reason than to demonstrate that Max was wrong, the continuing education office agreed to render whatever assistance it could. Max's face lit up with a sense of accomplishment and he soon excused himself, presumably to start work on the agreement. And work he did!

Within a week, a small, private, four-year religious college located nearby, advised that Max had talked them into offering a sophomore-level religion course, "The Life and Teachings of Jesus Christ," in extension on the community college campus. In itself, this was a major achievement because the small private college had only done this type of thing on very rare and special occasions in the past. And somehow, Max had gotten them to reconsider their policy and make an exception in this case. Perhaps the college officials were impressed by the fact that Max had already lined up one of their best professors to teach the course for no credit even if the college wouldn't sanction it. But even with official recognition, the college still specified that the Seekers would have to underwrite all costs for the course, including the professor's salary. But this didn't bother Max; he had already calculated the tuition rate he would have to charge to meet the cost of the course if he had to run it without college affiliation. Max's figures were pretty accurate too because he had already lined up twenty to thirty students to take the course.

The rest is all history of course. The class was held as scheduled and had a booming enrollment made up of a cross section of students and adult residents from the college community. And when it was over, they all clamored for more, including Max. Accordingly, the next semester, the college offered a continuing education class in "The Life and Teachings of Jesus Christ." It was also a success, as were many other subsequent attempts to serve the religious community.

While these successes made it look as if the Office of Continuing Education was doing a good job of analyzing and meeting the needs of the community, credit must be given where credit is due. None of these successful examples of serving the religious community would have ever come about if it had not been for the diligence and inspiration of Max. But the college was not the only one to benefit from this experience. Everyone who reads this account will have benefited from Max's example. It is to be hoped, then, they will join in saying, "Thank you, Mr. Rosenquist!"

The following example helps to illustrate some of the complexities and dynamics that evolve within a community college between continuing education and other academic divisions of the college. In this case study, there is evidence of operational difficulties; the resolution of competing interests can be a trying and sordid exercise.

The problem stems, of course, from the proclamation of territorial rights by each of the respective college departments or divisions. If a request has been made of the college to schedule a business law class off campus, what department should schedule and staff the course, the continuing education or the business department? While a cooperative endeavor is surely to be encouraged, that is more easily said than done! The business department might want the additional figures to bolster the justification for its staffing and budgeting allocations and requests. And then too, there is always the concern that if continuing education were to handle the matter, its selection of a staff member may not be so conscientious as that of the business department and a subsequently poorly taught course in this instance might reflect negatively on the entire business program at the college for years to come. Besides, the business department has the experienced faculty and syllabi ready at hand and could make preparations in response to this need on short notice with guaranteed quality(?).

On the other hand, it's the very mission of the continuing education department to respond to this kind of a request, and to bend to excessive articulation with the business department only detracts from the desired spontaneity. Agreed, everything will be done to vindicate the reputation of the college and the business department. After all, a sloppy job here would reflect as badly on the continuing education department as on the business program. And just because it's the continuing education department doesn't mean that its standards are any less than those of the rest of the college. Moreover, every effort will be made to use staff recommended by the business department. But if their professors are unwilling to go off campus, or teach nights, or release certain classes to be taught off campus, then the only result can be an inexcusable and indefensible inability of the college to respond in this situation.

Perhaps it is meaningful to recall, at this point, the occasion where one college was requested by a large military base nearby to offer programs to base personnel. The commanding officer and his top aides scheduled a meeting with the college president and his appropriate managers (including the chief administrators in the continuing education and the business department). The CO said, "We want a business program to be taught here. . . . I will guarantee you so many students. . . . We will pay the going extension tuition rate. . . . If that does not meet costs, we'll pick up the difference."

The college responded a few weeks later and advised that it would not be able to provide the service. Information from reliable sources reported that the business department faculty refused to allow or support the assignment of their programs or staff to that site. Nor would they sanction the courses with "resident status" credits if they were taught by instructors not associated with the department. Innuendo has it that the college administration was reluctant to act contrary to this position and hence the response to the CO was a disheartening no.

The following case study is certainly on a more positive note.

Serving the Health Care Community: A Case Study

As part of its continuing education program, William Rainey Harper College in Illinois has made every effort to serve the individual and corporate educational needs of the community as they are made known. In so doing, Harper College's Allied Health Division has developed and offered especially designed programs for given groups within the community, such as local businesses and industries, villages and townships, educators, and women's groups. Another identifiable community group which has evidenced a willing desire to take advantage of the educational opportunities available through Harper College has been the health-care community. Physicians, dentists, nurses, paraprofessionals, aides, secretaries and clerical assistants on the one hand, and clinics, hospitals, and convalescent centers on the other, have found that many if not all of their educational problems can be alleviated by working in close cooperation with their local community college. However, it hasn't always been that way.

History

For years, the hospitals found it logical, convenient, and expedient to train and upgrade their own staff. But with the advent of restraints upon their facilities, staffing, and budget, the hospitals found it more and more difficult to maintain existing in-house educational programs and to develop still others to keep their employees apace with changes and advances in the scientific and technical world. Moreover, the new equipment that was a product of the scientific and technical world and that was oftentimes not available for medical use was even more difficult to come by for training purposes. In the face of these and other problems that are typically associated with the day-to-day operation of a medical facility, it is easy to understand why members of the health-care community began to search for ways by which they could meet their occupational responsibilities and still not threaten their standards of professional quality. Of course, one of the most likely places to turn for such specialized educational assistance in the community is the community college.

Through its articulation and involvement with given community interest groups, Harper College became aware of the dilemma in its medical community. The college began to take steps that would provide it with the feedback needed to formulate programs that would help solve the educational problems of the health-care community. Health-occupation advisory committees were formed for these programs. College administrators began to attend and take an active part in the meetings of local and state medical organizations. Frequent contacts were initiated with local and respected officers of medical institutions. And as an important aside, the president of the college was appointed to the boards of directors of local hospitals. The product of this concerted effort was manifested in courses of study leading to certificates and degrees in all of the following:

1. Registered Nursing
2. Practical Nursing
3. Dental Hygiene

4. Medical Laboratory Technology
5. Operating Room Technology
6. Emergency Medical Training
7. Medical Transcription
8. Medical Office Assistance

In an effort to make these and other health occupations a part of a student's career-choice reservoir, a special class entitled "Health Occupations Orientation" was offered to acquaint potential students with the job opportunities available to them in the health field. In addition to these ongoing health career programs, there were still some educational needs of the medical community that were going unmet. Although these needs were just as important as those that had already been met, their unique nature indicated that they would be more appropriately satisfied by the office of continuing education.

Courses in pharmacology, medical terminology, and supervisory management were instituted to meet those particular needs. For various reasons, these courses were not available in other portions of the college curriculum. Moreover, each participating clinical agency had a slightly different angle of interest. Because the continuing education offices had more flexibility in developing programs to suit these divergent interests, the following approaches were utilized.

In the case of the medical terminology course, students from the medical community came with many different needs and expectations. Cassette tapes on medical terms were test-trialed in the course in an attempt to meet individual student needs. Each student could use the cassettes he or she found the most helpful. To meet the needs of students who required only limited exposure to a medical vocabulary, the course was scheduled for only eight weeks. (For those who needed advance and additional study, the course was scheduled for an additional eight weeks.) The students and teachers reported favorably on the use of the cassette tapes and of the abbreviated class length.

The establishment of the pharmacology course was one of the most difficult problems encountered. Each of the clinical agencies which had an interest in the course was invited to participate in meetings to develop the outline and content. One of the more frustrating factors was that each of the participating units had its own ideas as to just what should be included in the course. Compromising among these varying ideas and coordinating the practical laboratory experiences at the several medical units involved required enormous amounts of strategy and tact. The coordination problem was magnified even greater with regard to the supervisory management course.

Harper College and the community colleges of two adjoining college districts were approached by the North Suburban Association for Health Resources, to pool their resources and to provide a quality supervisory management program for the members and constituents of this organization. Coordinating the resources of the three colleges, the time schedules of their continuing education directors, and the needs and interests of fifteen medical institutions proved to be a frustrating task and tended to limit the degree of success in program development.

On a more positive note, however, Harper College was asked by one hospital within the community to provide a one-day seminar or workshop on management techniques. The continuing education office was quick to secure the services of a qualified management consultant and seminar leader and to so inform the hospital. The one-day program was well attended and with nary a hitch in planning the organization. The only drawback was that this type of format tended to be proportionately more expensive to put on and limited the extent to which the hospital budget could absorb future similar educational expenditures.

Observations

Persons in institutions who are preparing to embark upon the development of programs that are designed to serve the various staff, professionals, and institutions of the medical community would be well advised to get ready for a time-consuming and frustrating task. As are so many other lines of work, the medical field is becoming highly specialized. Accordingly, people in the health occupations represent a variety of interests, backgrounds, needs, and expectations. The number and level of problems that are generated by this multitude of differing traits are heightened even more by individual institutional priorities and perceptions. Add to these difficulties those of the varying educational budgets found amongst different medical agencies and units, plus the need for specialized facilities and equipment, and finally the mind-boggling problem of geographical logistics, it is not difficult to understand why the coordination of a comprehensive and sound health-careers program requires a monumental effort from all parties concerned.

Extensive planning and maximum participation from the medical community in the developmental processes can help to alleviate many of these problems. It is most helpful if the representatives at the developmental meetings are practitioners of the subject matter at hand. Administrators who attempt to speak for the specialists on their staff only tend to stifle the planning efforts. In spite of all the precautions one could take, the educational institution might still experience just as much or more success with a hastily organized program that is directed to meet a given request.

In this same vein, it should be remembered that a worthwhile educational activity for the medical community does not necessarily have to be a semester in length or for college credit. Except in those cases where a class is needed to satisfy current degree or certificate requirements, many of the health-occupations' needs can be met with short-term, one-shot seminars or workshops. While this approach might tend to be more expensive than a typical, ongoing class, in many instances it can qualify for funding from a growing number of federal and state grants for the health-careers field. Despite all of the difficulties facing the development and implementation of health-occupations programs, the medical community is bound together by its common interest in the field of medicine and its growing desire to seek the services of a qualified and respected educational agency. With this in their favor, educators who attempt to serve the medical community have every reason to hope for success.

4

Continuing Education Extended

One of the greatest things about continuing education is that it is always on the fringe of a new educational frontier—if, in fact, it is not the new educational frontier itself. Its recent past and unlimited future challenge its license to experiment and explore. For those who would consider continuing education as a serious career alternative, a creative and imaginative outlook are highly recommended traits. To perceive of the educational tomorrow is to pave the way for a more responsive and effective concept and program of continuing education. The following remaining pages of this text are a manifestation of this principle. They are this writer's prophecy of education, inclusive of continuing education, in the not-to-distant future. That continuing education may not be able to be distinguished from all education is by design, for it is suggested that continuing education and education will be one. Do you agree?

Universal Education

In writing about the nineteenth-century American concept of universal education, R. Freeman Butts, an educational historian, said "it was intended to provide equality of opportunity for everyone to go as far upward as his talents and abilities would take him." Furthermore, this opportunity should be available at "public expense under state auspices, and should begin at the lowest levels and extend through the university . . . . Secondary education would be a continuation of elementary education and higher education would follow secondary education. . . . [it should be] free, non-secular, coeducational and compulsory."

In testimony to its widespread acceptance, the concept of universal education has remained throughout the years as a guiding light to educators, politicians and students of the American social system everywhere. That the concept still prevails can be detected from a recent political convention where a plank in a party platform endorsed education as "an opportunity for every person to become whatever he or she was capable of becoming."

To this extent, then, the concept of universal education can and still does exist. And few would argue that the principles and aims of universal education are as righteous and well-founded as could be. It does not follow, however, that a nineteenth-century concept of education should continue as the basis for the twentieth-century educational design. Times and people have changed and so too their educational needs. In most cases, the concept of universal education still applies. But to make it functional in this age of astronauts and aquanauts, it must be updated and tuned in to the newfound capabilities of twentieth-century man.

A review of the literature clearly indicates that there is no inspiration or reference point for building a revised impression of universal education. Apparently, educators are relatively content with their current philosophical underpinnings and see no need to review their pedagogical rhetoric vis-à-vis the changing times. Therefore, the search must go beyond the educational void and into other areas of study and knowledge. One of the most promising, yet most ignored, collection of ideas that can be found is in the realm of science fiction.

While the annals of science fiction rarely, if ever, devote their pages to the concerns of education, they do provide the incentive for exciting dynamics and creative thought. But because of its fictional basis, most educators are reluctant to pay science fiction the respect that it so rightfully deserves.

And for this same reason, the contribution that science fiction could conceivably make to education has barely been tapped.

Science Fiction

Jules Verne, Aldous Huxley, and George Orwell all have something in common. They were all venturesome enough to forecast social and scientific phenomena that were not beyond the bounds of reason. To this extent, these literary figures have made considerable contributions to the field of science fiction. Their names and works are certainly not household words, but their thoughts and prophecies have left a lasting impression upon thousands of learned and lay minds alike. While they probably cannot be classified with the likes of Shakespeare, Hemingway, or Eliot, these authors can certainly be credited with causing their followers to think about tomorrow. Who in the day of Verne would have read of submarine and spaceship travel and not have wondered if it would ever come about? And if it did, what would it mean for man, his life, and his environment?

Who has read of the year *1984* or of the *Brave New World* and not pointed an accusing finger at the contemporary authority symbol and labeled it "Big Brother"? How much imagination does it take to associate the police and military handlings of civil rights demonstrations in the 1960s with the predictions of a police state? But, of course, this analysis could go on and on. The point is that science-fiction authors have made some alarming predictions of the world to be. Were man to have paid closer attention to their writings, he might have paved the way for the more graceful arrival, or if need be, the utter repudiation and defeat of, developments that the not-too-distant future holds in store.

Perhaps if man had begun to develop an appreciation of the concept of space travel from the time that Jules Verne first wrote of it, he would not be so confused about its relatively high budget priority in the face of other, apparently more pressing, national concerns. It is to be hoped that because of Orwell's allusion to the existence of a police state within the next few decades, man will have taken every precaution to guard against a political system that controls rather than inspires the free will and actions of its constituents.

Of course, these are only a couple of examples of how science fiction could have eased the growing pains of mankind. But if nothing else, it certainly demonstrates the far-reaching potential of science-fiction thought. To this extent, education could benefit from a science-fiction analysis of its future image. The writing is already on the wall. Education will and must change to meet the dynamic demands of a highly technical tomorrow.

As evidence, one needs merely to consider the widely unknown fact that the world is resounding in shock waves of concussion proportionate to the knowledge explosion. While the magnitude of the explosion has been felt in every corner of the earth and beyond, it has amazingly not caused the slightest tremor in academia. As usual, educators are not prepared to deal with a knowledge explosion. In their conservative, heel-dragging fashion, they have failed to do anything approaching the dynamic in meeting the demands of the knowledge explosion and the educational challenges it presents for tomorrow. Undoubtedly, one author hit the nail on the head when he candidly observed "that on the average, it takes educators twenty-five years to implement the findings of their research. And by that time, it is out of date." If educators are going to successfully confront the challenges of the knowledge explosion, they would do well to project the analysis of their dilemma beyond today and onto tomorrow. If the accuracy of the predictions of Verne, Orwell, and Huxley are any indication, then it might be of value to experiment with the medium of science fiction.

The Knowledge Explosion

John W. Gardner, former secretary of the Department of Health, Education, and Welfare, once admonished that, "We should stop this increasingly silly fiction that education is for youngsters and devise many more arrangements for lifelong learning. Education is a lifelong process." Mr. Gardner is one of a growing number of social critics throughout the world today who have recognized that the time has come for us to begin to develop a system of education that meets the needs of all men throughout all of life. We are swiftly approaching the time in the evolution of our civilization when a person can no longer think of ever completing the learning process.

Julius Robert Oppenheimer, the nuclear physicist of atom-bomb fame, was apparently well aware that this need for continuing education existed. He once reported to an audience that much of what he knows today was not in a book ten years ago. These words of caution from an intellect of Mr. Oppenheimer's caliber certainly draw some much needed attention to the need for lifelong learning.

A Call to Arms

In the face of this glaring reality, apparently nothing is being done about the knowledge explosion. For example, consider the findings of a study conducted by the National Opinion Research Center over a decade ago. At that time N.O.R.C. reported that only about one-fifth of the adult population was pursuing some kind of formal or informal continuing education. Based on these findings and with a generous allowance for statistical error, it is reasonably safe to conclude that as many as 50 percent of the population are not keeping up with the knowledge explosion. Alarming as these facts might sound, there is no reason to believe that this same problem is not being experienced by other planets in other galaxies in other solar systems. Who is to say that there are not John W. Gardners, Julius R. Oppenheimers, and professional educators and researchers in these unknown reaches who have also warned their constituents of the impending need to continually pursue the learning process?

But recognizing the existence of the knowledge explosion and alerting the citizenry of its need to prepare for it is only part of the problem. A revision and revamping of the existing educational system to meet the challenge of the knowledge explosion must also be taken into account. And herein probably lies the greatest chore; for if two partners were ever inseparable, they are education and tradition. In fact, tradition is probably one of the big reasons why it takes educators twenty-five years to implement their out-of-date research findings.

If there is only a grain of truth to this remark, it is ground enough for launching a monumental effort to meet the challenge of the knowledge explosion. Halfhearted manipulations are not the answer. Rather, a much more significant effort must be made to revise our educational system. This revision must come immediately. It must be as concerted and farsighted as the efforts that have produced magnificent and heretofore unknown tools such as radar and synthetic materials. It must be an effort that goes beyond the boundaries of the local school district, beyond the state superintendent of instruction, beyond the Department of Health Education and Welfare, and that somewhat approaches the omnipotence of the United Nations. It must be an effort that takes budgetary priority over the financing of wars and their implements of death and destruction. It must be an effort that is in concert with our current efforts at exploring the ocean floors and the planets in our solar system. It must be an effort that is concerned with providing the most meaningful, productive, expedient, cosmopolitan, and futuristic educational system imaginable. It must be a system of quality education for all characterized by success and achievement rather than by punishment and failure. It must lay the basis for our lives of tomorrow—lives that will extend far beyond the limits of our earthly existence. It must, in the last analysis, be the catalyst for a system of universal education. A system that will assume characteristics totally unfamiliar to us. Characteristics not unlike those of the world of Reld Jorn.

Pass the Smart Pills, Please

Reld Jorn is the man of tomorrow. He breathes, sleeps, and eats knowledge. He begins and ends each day with an intelligence cocktail and two smart pills. While at rest, he is linked to a self-energized unit that is forever receiving and sending knowledge as it occurs throughout the universe. During his waking hours, Reld consumes food prepared under knowledge rays, drinks water from a city reservoir treated with knowledge chemicals, and breathes air enriched with knowledge molecules. Reld does not exist today but he will by the year 2000.

• • •

"For crying out loud, that's the third time I've tried that tape. One more time and that's it. If I don't get it then, I'm going to try celestial gerontology!"

Reld Jorn tore the ear-jacks from his head, bolted from the bed and (in light of his recent failure) planned his next career move as he scurried about the kitchen in search of nourishment. WHIRrrrr the blender was mixing a barf-colored concoction that was a lot more productive and healthy than tasty.

"Yuck! If I didn't need this 'smart' cocktail, I wouldn't touch the damn stuff. But it's sure to help me whip the submarine masonry program the next time out!"

What a shame—Reld's disappointing career efforts, that is. After all, he had been afforded every conceivable opportunity to become whatever he was capable or desirous of becoming. At conception, he was a product of his mother's and father's combined intelligence. Throughout gestation, his mother consumed drugs, foods, liquids, and took mechanical treatments that had imparted the quantified elements of knowledge on his behalf.

Every waking and sleeping childhood hour was spent linked, mechanically or with mental telepathy, to the Knowledge Module—a self-maintaining, modified planetoid that had been outfitted with millions of antennae to receive, permanently store, and disseminate all knowledge that ever would and even could occur. And when that wasn't enough, Reld could spend some time at a regional learning center to practice controlled H-bomb explosions, journey back in time to witness the creation of earth, or just practice his interpersonal skills with the crystal-shaped residents of Uranus.

When firsthand points of history or fact were needed, he could always communicate with persons whose physical presence had ceased to exist. Fingering the terminal keyboard in between sips and munches of knowledge-rich food and drink, Reld's mind reminisced with the thoughts and words of parents and others who had gone before him. He responded to the display on the terminal screen and chuckled to himself.

"To think that things like grades, degrees, teachers, counselors, administrators, students, and schools once existed. And here I am, cultivated and nurtured for learning before and after birth; exposed and compelled to every conceivable learning device and technique throughout life and destined to continue the acquisition of knowledge after death."

"Can you beat that?" he muttered. "All of that time, expense, money (whatever that was), that used to go into education and here I am accomplishing all of that and more while I'm eating breakfast! Now you'ld think with all of that going for me, I wouldn't be having so much trouble getting through that submarine masonry program!"

"How ironical," he thought, "we've got complete and total mastery of the chemistry, technology, and devices of learning, and we still haven't got a good handle on individual learning processes."

"Well, back to the Knowledge Module, Module, Module, Module, dumule, emuuldm, e .. mod .. l d-*#mou#.L#,dk3'$&*." . . . . EMERGENCY REPAIR . . INDICATED . . ANDROID MODEL 610 SERIAL NUMBER 1210x R. Jorn.

• • •

Reld was and is of tomorrow. His coming may or may not be as imminent as the devices which will assuredly signal his arrival, devices such as the Knowledge Module.

The Knowledge Module

The Origin

Today's scientific probes to the depths of the ocean floor and to the planets within our solar system are but a prelude to what the years ahead will hold in store. Eventually, it will be a common place for man to dwell in a subterranean as well as a submarine world. Likewise, man's extraterrestrial mobility will develop to the point where interplanetary travel and residence will be customary throughout the entire universe. To complement man's expanded geographical identity, a cosmopolitan educational system will evolve that will be designed to equip him for life within the expanse of the universe and all of its farthest reaches. This system and all of its pedagogical elements are the ingredients of a phenomenon hereinafter referred to as universal education.

Educational Immortality

In the next millenium, continuing one's education throughout life will become as essential to the well-being of the organism as food, air, and water is today. Knowing how to adjust the physiological self from the subterranean environment of the planet Mars to the terrestrial atmosphere of the earth's moon might conceivably be a bit of life-or-death information for the cosmopolitan man of the year 3000. To enable a person to keep up with items such as this in particular, and the knowledge explosion in general, education will truly become a perpetual process—a process that will begin before birth and continue on after death.

Prior to conception, the father and mother-to-be will be gorging themselves with the proper nutrients, vitamins, and other chemical substances to insure the production of a fetus that is of maximum intelligence and learning ability. At conception, it is well within reason that parents might have the capability of passing along their combined intelligence, not just the hereditary inclination, unto the unborn child via the act of sexual intercourse. Should the act of sexual intercourse ever be replaced by other means of psychophysical stimulation, test-tube babies could conceivably be the product of especially selected parents, bathed in solutions that insure an offspring of optimum intelligence and ability.

One university professor has already addressed himself to this possibility. He suggests that the sperms and ova of individuals possessing desirable intellectual (and other) traits will be produced on a systematic basis. As the desired sperms and ova are produced, they will be preserved for laboratory mating under favorable conditions. Implicit in the professor's suggestions is that genetically undesirable persons will not be permitted to reproduce offspring. As a matter of expediency, it would probably be most advantageous to render these people impotent at birth. While these measures would probably be a significant step towards the development of a superior intellectual race of beings, they would undoubtedly raise moral issues of far-reaching concern. But whether or not selective breeding should become a wave of the future, it will not preclude the fact that the act of learning will never cease.

Following the preconception and conception stages, learning will continue throughout birth and infancy. Just as today's newborn child is given medicines to guard against certain infectious diseases, so too will the baby of the future be given drugs to preserve the intelligence it has acquired and to insure its continued growth. Learning will continue throughout the childhood and adult years causing the intellectual line of demarcation between these two age groups to become severely blurred.

While the younger years will continue to emphasize the development of basic psychomotor skills and knowledge, and the older years the intellectual and cultural preparation for a vocation, in the next century, the content and complexity of the subject matter will be altered immensely from the kinds of learning experiences we associate with these age levels today.

Curriculum Continuum

Prenatal months	Likely to learn some psychomotor skills and basic knowledge
Younger years	Likely to experience cultural and intellectual enrichment
Older years	Likely to pursue vocational-related education
Postmortem years	Likely to maintain basic knowledge at a level commensurate with subsequent years

As has been indicated, the basic skills and knowledge needed to function in the years ahead will be, to a large degree, imparted via proper breeding, nutrition, and chemical treatment during the prenatal and natal days. But because the universal quantity and quality of knowledge will continue to grow like Topsy, the younger person will have to continually add to and develop his fundamental capabilities.

In place of or in supplement to, millions of written and spoken languages and their dialects that will be found throughout the universe, the younger person will probably want to master the universal tongue of mental telepathy. Although a conversational command of many languages will be helpful as the people of tomorrow emigrate about the universe, the ability to communicate without total reliance on the mastery of all spoken or written words will greatly facilitate the communication process.

In addition to acquiring and maintaining a command of the communicative processes, people of tomorrow will also want to develop their scientific and technical ability to maximize and proliferate the utilization and development of the highly mecahnized life and learning system of their time. For this will be a universe that thrives on the exploitation of cybernetics and manipulation of the forces of the universe.

Once man has gained a relative command of the basic skills and knowledge that he needs to live and grow in the universe, he will then move on to become more familiar with his own and other cultures. Familiarity with cultures throughout the universe will be a necessary companion to man's unlimited extraterrestrial mobility and increasingly varied social relationships.

Somewhere after he acquires the basic skills and knowledge of communications, science, and technology, but not necessarily before his exposure to the cultures of the universe, man will begin to pursue the first of many vocational choices. He might adjust his comparative cultural studies to coincide with contacts or relationships with inhabitants or elements of a given culture as they occur throughout his life pattern. Because science will have extended his life span beyond the age of one hundred, man will have the opportunity to meet many different peoples and hold many different jobs before he terminates his occupational career. He will have held many different jobs because the phenomenal growth of knowledge will obviate the need for most vocations after only a few years of their existence. Moreover, man's broadened intellectual capabilities coupled with the efficient learning methods, techniques, and devices of his time will enable him to acquire the information he needs to change careers with relative ease.

Even after his working days have ended, man will need to continue his education. Probably his most pressing concern will be to satisfy his thirst for intellectual stimulation. Having lived a life characterized by the constant acquisition of knowledge and skill, it will be necessary for his mental capacities to find acceptable substitutes and outlets to meaningfully occupy the remaining years. But just because the intensity of the learning process will have lessened, it by no means will ever cease. Upon death and in the hereafter, man will continue to learn. Although his physical presence might prove to be expendable, his mental prowess will remain throughout time.

His postmortem curriculum will consist of the continual development of communications skills so that he will forever be able to converse with the changing, living world. In so doing, he will forever be available to provide information and opinions of his time and person. He might, thereby, even obviate the need for the retention of cumbersome records and filing systems. Maintaining his skills and knowledge will also permit him minimal social adjustment problems when and if he should ever return to this or another living world in his former or a different physical presence. But whatever his mental or physical configuration, man will be secure in that he will have realized his respective life goals.

Goal Realization

Education of the future will be almost entirely learner-centered. Learning before and after the living years will be largely dictated by other persons, chemicals, or machines. Learning during the younger and older years will be actualized by the individual. Learning methods, techniques, and devices will be readily available and convenient to use. Job choice and change will occur frequently and will begin at an early age. Consequently man's educational needs will be satisfied as they occur. At one point in his life, he may study the science of spacial geology and the culture and terra firma of Saturn. Three years later, he may pursue a career in marine life of the canals of Mars.

Because learning will necessarily occur as the learner demands, dividing the learning system into ascending levels of instruction would be meaningless. Man will not have the time nor the need to matriculate through the various levels of degrees or diplomas and all of their dubious requirements. He must have the opportunity to learn at his own rate of speed and not as some institution or teacher requires. The tempo of his times will not permit him to follow a laborious and time-consuming path of grades one through twelve or degrees such as the bachelor's, master's, or doctorate. Nor will the tempo of his times allow irrelevant course prerequisites or examinations. He will pursue a given body of knowledge as he sees fit. If he lacks the proper background for acceptable comprehension of a given subject, he will, of his own accord, return to a program of study that will provide him with the information that he needs to proceed further in his current educational track.

Man will not be punished nor will he experience failure to achieve minimal learning goals. He will pursue his set of learning objectives until he achieves the necessary knowledge to realize his life goals. The only real limiting factor in his goal-realization will be his individual determination and perserverance. Man will not be marked for posterity with an impersonal letter symbol indicating an arbitrary degree of achievement and administered by a person who cannot begin to relate to the motivations and expanded educational needs of a person's universal existence.

To support this dynamic and learner-centered program of instruction, there will necessarily be developed a correspondingly unique system of education. This system will have the capability of dispensing knowledge at any time and probably in almost any place. It will have to be a system that is as up-to-date as tomorrow and as versatile and flexible as the people that it will serve. It must be a pedagogical entity of such omnipotence and high regard that its ability to substitute for the sacrosanctness of grades, teachers, and degrees can never be questioned. In the final analysis, it must be the center of all knowledge. And for want of a better term, it shall be known as the Knowledge Module.

The focal point for all learning in future generations will be the Knowledge Module. Quite simply stated, the function of the Knowledge Module will be to collect and disseminate knowledge, including psychomotor skills, throughout the universe. An added feature of the Knowledge Module, to be discussed under later headings, will be the maintenance of the financial support system for universal education.

The Knowledge Module will collect and disseminate knowledge through an extremely intricate network of sensory mechanisms. These sensory mechanisms will have the unique ability to focus on and attract and store all new knowledge as it occurs within the universe. This function of monitoring and storing all new knowledge may be effected by equipping the Knowledge Module with trillions upon trillions of extremely sensitive sending and receiving antennae.

At the outset, the Knowledge Module will probably have to be fed all of the existing knowledge to bring it up to date. This initial information-gathering will of course require a monumental cooperative effort of all of the constituents of the universe. But after surmounting this initial hurdle, the Knowledge Module will be well on its way to being the educational savior of all. Its subsequent efforts need merely concern themselves with maintaining existing knowledge as it occurs.

Correspondingly, every living unit (i.e. homes, apartments, underwater cells, space satellites) throughout the universe will be equipped with learning subsystems that can be directed to send and retrieve information to the Knowledge Module. The sophisticated learning subsystems will be as common to the household of tomorrow as the telephone is today. Moreover, they will have a myriad of capabilities.

Upon receipt of information from the Knowledge Module, the home learning subsystems will be able to convert the knowledge to visual or audio format. If the person so desires, the information may also be converted to telepathic wavelengths that could transmit knowledge to the organism's mental processes while it rests or while it is engaged in some other form of activity. Another function of the learning subsystems would be to augment the sensory antennae of the Knowledge Module by comprising an extensive network of relay stations for gathering new knowledge. The Knowledge Module will also be responsible for evaluating performance levels that are necessary to pursue given life goals. This responsibility will be intricately interwoven with the instruction system to the extent that it will never be detected. The Knowledge Module will integrate this evaluation system along with other instructional techniques (i.e. reinforcement, repetition, and so on), to such an extent that the learner will never realize that he is being evaluated. Rather, he will only experience continued progress and success.

In order to serve the inhabitants throughout the entire universe, the Knowledge Module will necessarily have to be a centrally located planetoid or manmade satellite. If it is a planetoid, it will have been selected for its function because it has the proper composition and characteristics that will lend themselves to being manipulated into this highly intricate learning device. If a planetoid with the proper qualifications cannot be found, the scientific and technological wisdom of the universe will be brought together in a cooperative effort at engineering and constructing an artificial satellite of the proper proportions and functional requirements. In addition to the Knowledge Module and the home-based learning systems, universal man will also have ready access to regional learning centers.

Regional Learning Centers

Regional learning centers will house educational devices that are too cumbersome and expensive for the home. The centers will also serve as places where laboratory, psychomotor, and vocational skills can be practiced. After all, in spite of the Knowledge Module's fantastic simulation capabilities, it would certainly not be practical for it to reproduce a learning experience that is beyond the physical limitations of a person's living unit. For example, a person's living room could hardly accommodate a reproduction of the first atom smasher or similiar bulky entities. The Knowledge Module and the regional learning centers will not, however, be the sole means of facilitating the learning process. They will be amply augmented with a variety of learning aids and approaches that will promote a successful learning process.

Methods, Techniques, and Devices

The major method of learning will probably be self-study via the Knowledge Module. Where a chosen vocation requires a skilled proficiency, internships will remain as a necessary instructional method; however, the use of internships will be greatly lessened by the markedly improved ability of the individual to acquire from the Knowledge Module the needed information to improve his skills performance. To some extent, the laboratory method will still exist as an opportunity for the individual to practice and refine knowledge and skills. But because of the ability of the Knowledge Module to provide real-life simulations and because of its ability to evaluate a person's reaction to them, the need for laboratories will be severely limited. After all, why should a chemistry experiment with explosive elements be attempted when the procedures and resulting mixture or solution can all be mechanically communicated to and evaluated for success by the Knowledge Module?

Compared to those of today, the techniques of universal education will differ more in quality than they will in kind. Even though the primary educational method will be self-study with the Knowledge Module as a tutor, the Knowledge Module will also be able to lecture on its own and to reproduce those of the most learned and noted men that have ever spoken. The need for reading as a technique will diminish as alternative means of assimilating knowledge are refined and put into practice. After all, there really is not much need to

**Facilities of
the Learning Network**

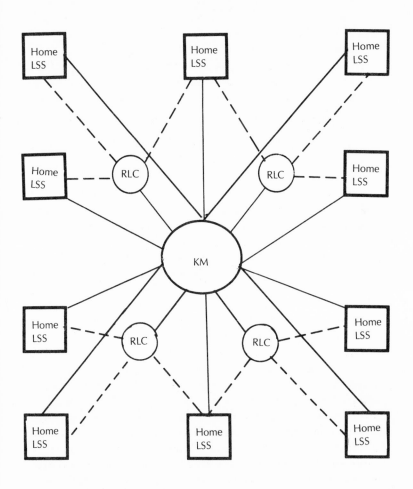

KM   = Knowledge module
RLC = Regional learning center
H LSS = Home learning subsystem

pore over an endless collection of letter symbols if the knowledge can more easily be chemically or mechanically assimilated while the person is at rest or pursuing other activities.

The Knowledge Module will also be able to debate with its user and to contrive and evaluate drills for the learner as the need arises. The technique of demonstrating, via audiovisual means, will be a normal ancillary activity of the Knowledge Module's everyday function of dispensing information. Hardly a word or telepathic wave will be uttered that is not illuminated with a demonstration.

The techniques of role playing and field trips will take on added dimensions in the universal system of education. Because of a time-space-dimension machine, man will be able to take field trips back into time to observe firsthand a notable historical development. He will also be able to transfer his person at a moment's notice from his own time and place to that of another location in the universe to witness or participate in a social movement in progress. And if he is so inclined, the time-space-dimension machine will also be able to project the individual into the future to follow up his study of a given phenomena and pursue it to its logical and ultimate conclusion.

Universal man's ability to transplant himself to any point in the past, present, or future will also make for meaningful role playing. In this case, the experience will not have to suffer from many of the inaccuracies of role playing because the person will be able to participate in the actual event itself. Of course, there will have to be limitations as to the participant's role. Such safeguards would be necessary to insure that the history and time relationships would not be seriously altered to the extent that they might cause a raging chaos of historical evolution. If this extension of an approach to role playing is not needed to meaningfully illustrate a given educational point, then the learner can interact with the Knowledge Module itself because another one of its many capabilities will be to assume more than one character in a role-playing situation. An added feature of the time-space-dimension machine will be its ability to transform man into the role of characters in literary and artistic creations. How better to understand the message of an author or an artist than to relive his characters as he portrayed them?

An interesting variation on the field-trip technique and the laboratory method will occur as man perfects his ability to control, at will, the size of his own and other physical entities. While it is indeed helpful to be able for modern man to magnify things of a microscopic nature to the extent where individuals can observe them in a visible size (as we do with a microscope today), it might be just as meaningful for man to be able to reduce his physical stature to a point where he is comparable in size to that of a microscopic organism. In so doing, he could tour the protons of a cell's nucleus or study a cell's structure as he navigates himself about the protoplasm.

In spite of these and other advanced techniques of instruction, man will still be hard-pressed to keep up with the growth rate of knowledge. Accordingly, more convenient and even less time-consuming techniques will be developed to complement the learning process. In the thrust of this vast scientific progress, future man will perhaps be able to identify the very basic components of knowledge. To the extent that they can be identified, they will be reproduced in quantity and interspersed with consumable liquids, foodstuffs, and the atmosphere and, hence, be absorbed into the person as he is eating, drinking, or breathing. As the phenomenon of knowledge becomes more and more quantifiable, the delivery devices of information will necessarily become more sophisticated.

It is highly unlikely that universal education will waste the time, space, or money to produce, store, and use such things as films, blackboards, projectors, television, and so on. Because they will already be an intricate part of the Knowledge Module and its learning network, the instructional role of audiovisual resources will be maximized.

As complete and productive as the methods, techniques, and devices of universal education will be, they are not the panacea for all of education's ills. The most significant problem that must be resolved by universal educators will be the exact operation of the learning process and all of its mental complexities. By identifying the elements and their interrelationship with the whole organism in effecting changed behavior, universal man will be able to maximize the learning capabilities of all living things and, hence, enable them to keep up with the knowledge explosion. The discovery of the elements and operation of the learning process will probably be greatly dependent upon the extent to which universal man is able to reveal and to capitalize upon the many untold secrets and unused capabilities of the brain.

As the evolution of the Universal System of Education approaches fruition, a corresponding change in the vocabulary of education will come to pass. At the same time that many terms are falling into disuse, a whole batch of new ones will come into play.

Vocabulary

It is difficult to predict, with any degree of certainty, what new words will come about with the advent of universal education. Scientists and technicians of all disciplines have a peculiar knack for coining a lingo unbeknownst to the lay citizen. And because the educational scheme of tomorrow will be highly steeped in science and technology, the new vocabulary that ensues, will be, in all likelihood, correspondingly unique. This prediction is not without precedent. Merely reconsider the works of Jules Verne.

Mr. Verne wrote of submarines and spaceships with amazing insight but he could hardly conceive of such twentieth-century terms as EVA (Extra Vehicular Activity) and LEM (Lunar Excursion Module). And by the same token, it is similarly difficult to foretell the pedagogical jargon of tomorrow. Although it is admittedly difficult, if not impossible, to predict the educational vocabulary of tomorrow, crystal-balling the terms and phrases that will probably fall into disuse can be done with a greater degree of certainty. One good example is the word "student." Because of the ever increasing growth rate of knowledge, people will necessarily continue the learning process throughout life. Since everyone will be a student and that word will no longer differentiate one person from another, there will be no need for the term. To call universal man a student would be like calling contemporary man an eater, breather, or drinker because he consumes food, air, or water.

Terms such as teacher, professor, and counselor are also probably destined for extinction. The Knowledge Module and the sublearning systems will shoulder the bulk of the instructional and guidance workload with minimal assistance from the Regional Learning Centers. If these terms exist at all, they will be associated with the Knowledge Module and its related systems.

As indicated, educational counseling and guidance will be another feature of the Knowledge Module. If a warm and understanding face is considered to be an essential ingredient of a given counseling relationship, the Knowledge Module will be able to simulate or transmit one via its audiovisual capabilities. During the transition period before the universal systems of education reaches fruition, man will undergo a period of adjustment in getting used to his technical and automated environment. If person to person contact is a must during this period of adjustment, the Regional Learning Center will offer the services of superbly trained and qualified professionals. Eventually, however, time will reveal the disappearance of educational counselors and the term designating that profession.

Just as the terms student, teacher, professor, and counselor become passé, so too will the words principal, superintendent, dean, and president. The basic learning unit or universal education will be the home with its sublearning system hookup to the Knowledge Module. Since there will be no schools as such, there will be no need for administrators to manage them. And because there will be no administrators, there will be no need for words to reflect their existence.

The educational needs for universal man will demand a curriculum that permits him access to learning at the time and place he so desires. The educational needs of universal man will not allow his motivations to be hamstrung with such ridiculous hurdles of having passed first, second, and twelfth grades. Nor will universal man have to achieve given letter grades such as A, B, C, or D in a compulsory course of study. Moreover, the great number of career changes and the growth of knowledge that will occur during his life span will no longer warrant the need for a bachelor's degree in this, a master's degree in that, and a doctorate in something else. By universal education, standards, universal man will have earned fifteen to twenty postdoctoral degrees, each in a different field of study, before his physical being expires. What is more, the body of knowledge will have changed so fast that whatever universal man could have learned to satisfy the requirements of a degree would soon be outdated.

Based on this account, there would appear to be little need for words that signify levels of education, letter grades, and pieces of paper indicating supposed mastery of a given body of subject matter. With no schools, grades, degrees, teachers, and administrators, terms that identify the different levels of education would also disappear. "Kindergarten," "elementary schools," "junior high schools," "high schools," "colleges," and "universities" are a few of the words that will become as archaic as hieroglyphics. Likewise there will no longer be a need for the word "library." No library in the universe could ever begin to store the wealth of knowledge that will be found in the Knowledge Module. And as libraries fall into disuse, so too will the word that connotates their existence.

These are but a few of the words that will probably disappear from the educational vocabulary of universal man. The reader can surely think of more. But he is cautioned not to interpret the demise of such a large part of the contemporary pedagogical vocabulary to mean that universal education will want for lack of substance and organization. Quite the contrary, the awesome capabilities of the Knowledge Module will necessitate a highly centralized and efficient system of governance.

Organizations

In spite of the perpetual claims that the proliferation of an educational bureaucracy only breeds graft, corruption, warbled communication, and higher costs, it will persist in the educational scheme of tomorrow. But because of an almost entirely new set of parameters, the management and organization of the Universal System of Education will circumvent or at least minimize the number of pitfalls normally attributed to an educational bureaucracy or any other bureaucracy for that matter. One of the reasons for this prediction of a streamlined and more efficient bureaucracy is based upon the greatly expanded life-style of universal man.

The educational experiences of universal man will be a manifestation of his extremely expanded environment. The contents and composition of his cosmopolitan curriculum will be ably imported via the Knowledge Module. Because of its seemingly never ending capabilities, the Knowledge Module will be, without a doubt, the heart of universal education. The proper and perpetual operation of the Knowledge Module will therefore be as necessary to the perpetuation of the universe as insulin is to the diabetic. Even if the most minor malfunction should go unattended for even the briefest of moments, it could cause irreparable calamities of catastrophic proportions. Moreover, if the Knowledge Module were ever to come under the control of malicious or power-minded persons, it could be used to maim the mind of every universal resident. Such action could conceivably lead to the decay of the very socioscientific fabric that holds the universe together.

To guard against these and other eventualities, the various constituents of the universe will band together to form a governing body. In effect, and not without a lot of resistance, this new managerial system will replace the educational bureaucracy as we know it today. Where the opportunity permits, the bureaucrats of the current educational model will be recycled into the new educational design. In most instances, however, extensive retraining will be required to make these people operational in the highly scientific and technical world of tomorrow. Moreover, they will undoubtedly also have to undergo a sufficient period of reorientation to remove the many vestiges of their outdated concepts of education. As all of this develops, the new managerial system of education will be going about its business.

The primary function of the governing body will be to oversee the maintenance, operation, and protection of the Knowledge Module. Probably a good title for such an important organization would be The Universal Council on Education. In all likelihood, the Universal Council on Education will find it most appropriate to act in consort with the advice and consent of the representatives of the many cultural groups from the various galaxies, solar systems, planets, satellites, and submarine living units.

Allowing representatives from every corner of the universe to share in the governance will help to guard against the dominance and subsequent selfish manipulation of the Knowledge Module by any one group or person. In order to further guard against this possibility, it would probably be a good idea to rotate the membership of the Universal Council of Education among the many representatives to the governing body.

In addition to the Universal Council on Education, perhaps the only other educational managers involved might be the directors of regional educational centers. As the reader will recall, these centers will provide opportunities for experiences in laboratory, psychomotor, and social-interaction skills. More than likely though, the role of these directors should be more akin to that of technical supervisor than it would be to that of an educational manager.

Beyond the Universal Council on Education, its constituent representatives, and the directors of the regional centers, there would appear to be little further need for a managerial hierarchy. In view of this limited administrative structure, the management of education will experience a redefined role in terms of its lessened responsibilities in the universal system of education.

Organizational Structure

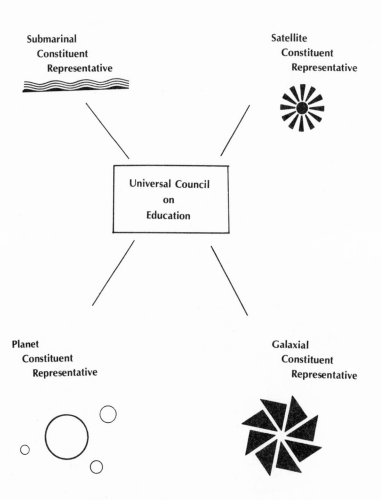

Submarinal
Constituent
Representative

Satellite
Constituent
Representative

Universal Council
on
Education

Planet
Constituent
Representative

Galaxial
Constituent
Representative

Administration

Because of the overwhelming ability of the Knowledge Module to absorb so many of the educational functions, most of the worries of contemporary educational administrators will not exist. Because there will be no board of trustees, no faculty, virtually no facilities, except for the Knowledge Module and regional learning centers, the administrator of tomorrow will not have to be concerned with multiplicity of meetings, staffing, unions, and buildings and grounds. His educational problems will be greatly narrowed in scope. They will deal almost exclusively with the Knowledge Module and related problems and issues. The awesome responsibility of tending to the Knowledge Module will more than compensate for the lightened administrative work load.

Administrators will continue to make decisions, especially regarding the maintenance and security of the Knowledge Module, the sublearning systems and the regional learning centers. Programming these decisions into a plan for implementation will be a function that will be absorbed, to a large extent, by scientifically advanced computerized systems. Developing and implementing alternative plans and evaluating their consequences will become a minor administrative responsibility. Computerized systems will reach such a degree of sophistication that they reduce this managerial chore to a menial, effortless, and errorless task.

Once the plan for implementation has been determined, managers of the Universal System of Education will, as their predecessors, continue to communicate the plan to all who must carry it out. But because the administrative hierarchy will be significantly less in size and number than it is today, communication will be less of a problem than today. For these very same reasons, the supervision and evaluating problems of the communication process will be correspondingly lessened. It can be assumed that the basic principles of educational administration will probably not change, but there is every reason to believe that the number of operational problems will dwindle and be replaced by a corresponding amount of increased managerial responsibilities. One of the biggest reasons for this altered managerial role will be the fact that there will be fewer physical facilities to maintain.

Facilities

Except for those occasions where an individual will need to use some of the specialized equipment and facilities of the regional learning centers, a person's residence will serve as his school. Through its linkup with the Knowledge Module, the home will become the place where most learning will occur. Because the home will be the primary learning unit, there will be no need for schools as we know them today. Consequently, most of the administrative problems that are typically associated with managing instructional buildings will be alleviated.

An incidental and not too burdensome building-management task will exist in the maintenance of the Knowledge Module and its home-based sublearning systems. A more familiar building management function will exist in the maintenance of the regional learning centers. The care and well-being of these facilities will be minimal, however, as universal man develops self-maintaining physical structures. Floors, walls and ceilings will be built of indestructible materials that dissolve, absorb, and recycle dirt, litter, and stain. Circulatory systems will not only heat and cool, but will also remove all dust, pollens, odor, and bacteria from the air. Where technical malfunctions arise in this and other specilized equipment, trouble lights will be triggered at the Knowledge Module operation center. Alerted to the malfunction, a competent technician will be dispatched to the wounded facility and the problem will be corrected posthaste.

In spite of these predictions, the preoccupation of educators to build instructional monuments in the name of academia will persist. But the effort to construct traditional facilities to meet the demands of the dynamic knowledge explosion will prove futile. Eventually these futile efforts will give way to the evolution of the Universal System of Education, and the respective cultures of the universe will be confronted with converting the remaining educational physical plants into useable facilities or razing them to the ground. In the event that the former course of action is chosen, some possible uses for the former educational structures might be:

1. Memory banks and/or informational retrieval linkages for the Knowledge Module.
2. Regional learning centers.
3. Centers for social and interpersonal growth and development.
4. Historical relics and/or museums of educational memorabilia and artifacts.

Whatever their fate, the continued operation of these facilities and their universal replacements will depend, as always, upon a viable system of finance.

Finance

The maintenance and operation of the universal system of education will not go without cost. As in twentieth-century educational operations, it will be necessary to develop a financial support system for universal education, one that is in keeping with the times.

Monetary levies on persons and properties will not be the mode of financing tomorrow's education. Rather, a universal education will be supported by a financial system that is as comprehensive as the educational system itself.

Because everybody will be a learner and hence a user of the educational system, everybody will contribute to its continued support and operation. While their contributions might not take the form of dollars, marks, or rubles, they will nevertheless be the foundation for the perpetuation of the universal system of education.

In all probability, the precedent of monetary support for education will disappear with the abolition of lira, pesos, francs, and pounds as mediums of exchange. Universal man will have developed devices to replace monetary systems as we know them today. Such devices might measure the amounts of universal resources that a person expends each time he uses the universal educational system or any other entity or phenomenon of that aeon. Correspondingly, the device will probably also be able to measure a person's contributions to the resources of the universe in terms of patients cured, research performed, spaceships repaired, homes built, and so on. It only stands to reason that a bookkeeping feat of this magnitude would obviously require an accounting system of tremendous proportions. Without a doubt, some sort of balance will have to be maintained. Such a document might logically be called the Master Balance Sheet.

The Master Balance Sheet on everyone's life will probably be of such complexity that it will require its own computer base of operations. But because it will be linked with so many other facets of the universe, i.e. education, retail stores, etc., it will probably have direct linkages with their respective operations. For example, a person would probably be able to receive his personal educational balance sheet by merely requesting that information of the Knowledge Module. Moreover, the Knowledge Module might be able to provide, on request, a person's entire balance sheet, inclusive of education and all other resources that he has expended and contributed.

Each person will be allowed a given amount of credit on his Master Balance Sheet. Of course, contributions to the body of universal resources will add to the credit side of the ledger, whereas consumption of universal resources will be marked on the debit side of the ledger. As a person reviews his balance sheet, he will be able to determine if his current or planned utilization of resources will exceed the amount of resources that he has credited to his account.

If a person should exceed the amount of resources and credit extension available to him, businesses and other institutions that are intertwined with this financial system will automatically be notified of that person's bad credit rating and his inability to consume further universal resources at that time. At this point, a person's financial well-being will compel him to undertake steps that will lead to contributions to the body of universal resources. Where needed, extensions of credit will nourish a person through times of physical impairment, ill health, and other pitfalls, to continued economic self-sufficiency.

Occasionally, circumstances at a given point in a person's life will appear to be characterized by a greater consumption than contribution to universal resources. But it must be recalled that all forms of contributions to universal resources will be calculated into the Master Balance Sheet. For example, an infant will be consuming great amounts of knowledge and physical care but will be contributing perhaps even greater amounts of love and psychological security for his parents or guardians. Likewise, an aged person might be diffusing his accumulated years of wisdom and experience to such an extent that it more than compensates for any deficits on the debit side of his life's ledger.

Overall, the financial support system for universal education will not be a major educational issue. It will be so immersed in the total economic operation of the universe that it will not be readily discernible from the educational process as a whole. Likewise, the perfection of the Knowledge Module will overshadow whatever issues that might, from time to time, draw attention to the management of the Universal System of Education and its facilities.

In fact, the Universal System of Education will be such a magnificent and productive operation that the greatest issues will be those which surround its development. Escaping the shackles of tradition will undoubtedly incite inordinate amounts of controversy and criticisms. The task of successfully meeting this controversy and criticism can not be taken lightly. It must be attacked with all due vigor. The chances of rising victorious over the enemies of educational change can be greatly improved by laying the strategic groundwork. And with that, the fight to build a better educational tomorrow can begin.

The Origin of the Species

The Knowledge Module is more than just a figment of the author's imagination. It is an educated fabrication influenced by the wisdom of literary giants who have foretold with an astonishing degree of accuracy many of life's contemporary realities. It is a scientific-technical extension of what is being experimented with in a disappointingly few laboratories around the world. It is a projection of the ideas and statements of many of today's futuristic thinkers. It is the manifestation of current psychosocial trends and dilemmas as they are logically pursued into the future. It is an amalgamation of the gimmicks and paraphernalia that have adorned science-fiction-oriented minds for years. And finally, it is a composite of ideas borrowed from Hollywood films, paperback novels, and television programs.

By referring to these sources of information, the reader will have some very definite cues as to what the future of education could hold in store. By reacting in a positive manner to these cues, the way can be paved for a quicker acceptance and development of a futuristic system of universal education. To ignore these cues is to invite educational catastrophe. And quite frankly speaking, the turn of events in the world today is of such catastrophic proportions that it can hardly withstand another catastrophe.

Granted, the gist of this paper has been to suggest that there is a better way to go about this business of education. Implicit in this analysis is that little is being done to correct this predicament and that needed changes are long overdue. In all honesty, however, it must be admitted that some pretty significant and exciting steps have already been taken.

A Face-Saving Note

All is not bad that appears bad. Modern man has given some evidence that he is, after all, concerned about the low ebb in the current tide of educational affairs. In the face of recent severe economic restraints, he has been forced to devise several measures that provide for greater accountability of educational funds and resources. And at the same time, many of these measures have also permitted the development of programs that are more responsive to student needs and interests. A brief review of some of these two-pronged, stop-gap measures might help the reader to see why they might very well be the stepping-stones to the Universal System of Education.

External degrees, free universities, credit-by-examination, and credit for life experiences are all examples of two-pronged efforts at reducing the costs of education. By adopting these programs, a college or university can minimize facility and staff needs and expenditures. By the same token, these programs also permit a student to learn where, when, if, and how he sees fit.

In many instances, the instructional content is conveyed to the home by television (sublearning systems) and supplemented by occasional seminars at a central location (regional learning centers). Telephone companies are farther along than most realize in developing educational devices that are linked to audiovisual senders-receivers. Because these devices could be part of the telephone system, they could conceivably reach every home that has the proper equipment. While this is not of the sophistication of a Knowledge Module, it is certainly a step in the right direction.

With the advent of such things as computerized instruction and programmed self-instruction packages that maximize the use of audiovisual media, there is hope that modern man has begun to fathom the potential of a completely self-maintaining learning system such as the Knowledge Module. Likewise, there is some indication of movement towards a universal system of educational finance.

Students of school finance have no doubt heard of P.P.B.S. (Planned Programmed Budgeting System). The whole thrust of P.P.B.S. is, of course, an attempt to redefine the budgeting process to the point where as many facets as possible of the educational process can be held financially accountable for their operation. Following P.P.B.S. to its ultimate achievement would manifest a system whereby the individual learner is responsible for educational budgeting. This fact coupled with other developments such as deferred tuition, and so on, are factors which are paving the way for a universal system of educational finance as suggested earlier.

While the proponents and practitioners of these new educational movements are to be commended for their forward-looking zeal, their actions can only be considered as a first step. If man is to move on toward fulfilling the prophecy of a Universal System of Education, his efforts must not stop.

Imperatives of Our Times

Admittedly, the universal system of education or some facsimile thereof cannot be accomplished overnight. This statement is not, however, intended in any way to sanctify procrastination. If modern man is to make significant advances towards the aims and goals of universal education, it will be necessary for him to devote maximum amounts of time, research, and money to unmask the secrets and potential of the brain and of computer systems.

By exploring every nook and cranny of the brain and revealing all of its unknown workings, man will probably be able to exploit the untold powers of mental telepathy. Recent experiments with the relaxing effects of the brain's alpha and beta waves are but a prelude to what could really be done with the services of the mind. Initial studies of biofeedback indicate that educators would do well not to overlook the potential of this phenomenon. With this expanded research of the brain, perhaps the learning process will be reduced to its very basic elements. When this is achieved, perhaps the chemical influences upon the learning process can be isolated, identified, and reproduced in quantity. And then, knowledge in a test tube might soon be in the offing.

At the same time that modern man is making significant inroads into the mysteries of the mind, it is necessary that he complement these endeavors with a refined embellishment of present computer systems. If the Knowledge Module or any thing of its sort is to ever become a reality, this effort must become an imperative of our times. Likewise, if the Universal System of Education is ever to come into being, it will be because the achievement of these goals were imperatives of our times.

Epilogue

Universal Education, Reld Jorn and the Knowledge Module are the educational wave of tomorrow. Their realization is an imminent extension of community colleges, continuing education, behavioral objectives, women's programs, Mr. Rosenquist, and the like. They are void of the competing duplication of community services, community schools, continuing education, adult education, community education, and community development. They are potentially attainable in the near future and one of their launching pads will be the facilities, programs, and curriculum of continuing education in the community colleges.

Notes

Introduction

1 L. Matlin, *Movie Comedy Teams* (New York: Signet, 1974).
2 E. Harlacher, *The Community Services Dimension of the Community College* (Englewood Cliffs, N.J.: Prentice-Hall, 1969), pp. 11–15.
3 A. Burrichter, "Let's Bury the Hatchet, Adult Educators!" *Mountain/Plains Adult Education Journal*, March 1975, pp. 23–30.

Continuing Education and the Community College

1 G. Jensen, A. Liveright, and W. Hallenbeck, *Adult Education* (Chicago: Aldine, 1965), pp. x–xi.
2 J. Johnstone and R. Rivera, *Volunteers for Learning* (Chicago: Aldine, 1965), tables 2.4, 2.8.
3 "Night School," *Newsweek*, March 5, 1973, pp. 20, 81.
4 V. Adams, "Adult Education: Where the Bread and Action Are," *College Management*, April 1973, pp. 9–14.
5 James G. Abert, "Money for Continuing Education," *Change*, Oct. 1973, pp. 8–9.
6 Armond J. Festine, "A Study of Community Services in the Community Colleges of State University of New York," unpublished doctoral dissertation, Syracuse University, 1967, pp. 26–28.
7 Jack Fuller, "Survey of Community College, Community Service Funding Patterns," unpublished study, William Rainey Harper College, Fall 1973, pp. 1–10.
8 David Lundsburg, "Community College Community Services: Rhetoric or Reality?" *Adult Leadership*, Dec. 1973, pp. 201–04.
9 Jack Fuller, "The Bastard of Community College Education," *Community Education*, May 1972, pp. 26–28.

121

[10] David Lundsburg, "Community College Community Services."

[11] Robert L. Jacobson, "Colleges Are Not Meeting Needs of Adults," *Chronicle of Higher Education,* Feb. 5, 1973, pp. 6–7.

[12] The term "conminuing edvices" is considered synonymous with continuing education, community education, noncredit programs, adult education, and any other jargon that educators might want to attach to that portion of the community college curriculum.

[13] E. Harlacher, *The Community Services Dimension of the Community College* (Englewood Cliffs, N.J.: Prentice-Hall, 1969), pp. 11–15.

[14] James W. Thornton, Jr., *The Community Junior College* (New York: John Wiley & Sons, 1966).

[15] Armond J. Festine, "A Study of Community Services."

[16] Glenn Jensen, *Handbook of Adult Education* (London. The Macmillan Co., 1970).

[17] Clyde E. Blocker, Robert H. Plummer, and Richard C. Richardson, Jr., *The Two-Year College: A Social Synthesis* (Englewood Cliffs, N.J.: Prentice-Hall, 1965).

Foundations of Continuing Education

[1] Peter F. Drucker, *The Practice of Management* (New York: Harper & Row, 1954), pp. 119–23.

[2] Robert F. Mager, *Preparing Instructional Objectives* (Palo Alto, Calif.: Fearon Publishers, 1962), pp. 1–10.

[3] George S. Odiorne, *Management-By-Objectives* (New York: Pitman, 1965), pp. 3–26.

[4] Jack Fuller, "Continuing Education by Objectives," *Journal of Continuing Education and Training,* Dec. 1971, pp. 175–79.

[5] Wendell R. Sheets and Robert E. Hostetler, "How to Organize for EDSPECS Development," *Community and Junior College Journal,* April 1973, pp. 24–25.

Bibliography

Abert, James G. "Money for Continuing Education," *Change*, Oct. 1973, pp. 8–9.

Adams, V. "Adult Education: Where the Bread and Action Are," *College Management,* April 1973, pp. 9–14.

Becker, John W. "Architecture for Adult Education." Washington, D.C.: Adult Education Association, 1960.

Blocker, Clyde E.; Plummer, Robert H.; and Richardson, Richard C. Jr. *The Two-Year College: A Social Synthesis.* Englewood Cliffs, N.J.: Prentice-Hall, 1965.

Boocock, Sarane S., and Schild, E.O. *Simulation Games in Learning.* Beverly Hills, Calif. Sage Publications, 1968.

Burrichter, A. "Let's Bury the Hatchet, Adult Educators!" *Mountain/Plains Adult Education Journal,* March 1975, pp. 23–30.

Continuing Education in Action: Residential Centers for Lifelong Learning. New York: John Wiley & Sons, 1968.

Deegan, Arthur X. *Management By Objectives.* Clearwater, Fla.: Deegan and Associates, 1971.

Dewey, John. *Democracy and Education.* New York: Macmillan, 1916.

Dewey, John. *Experience and Education.* New York: Macmillan, 1938.

Digest of Development Guidelines for William Rainey Harper College. Boston: Arthur D. Little, 1966.

Directory of Consultants for Planning Adult Facilities and Environments. Washington, D.C.: American Education Association, 1973–74.

Drucker, Peter F. *The Practice of Management.* New York: Harper & Row, 1954.

Edwards, F., and Hyberger, H. "Settings Conducive to Adult Learning," *Adult Leadership,* May 1964, pp. 16–18.

Engelhardt, N. L., and Engelhardt, N. L., Jr. *Planning the Community School.* New York: American Book Company, 1940.

Festine, Armond J. "A Study of Community Services in the Community Colleges of State University of New York." Unpublished doctoral dissertation, Syracuse University, 1967.

Fuller, Jack. "The Bastard of Community College Education," *Community Education Journal*, May 1972, pp. 26–28.

Fuller, Jack. "Building for Adult Education," *International Journal of Career and Continuing Education*, Fall 1975, pp. 25–33.

Fuller, Jack. "Continuing Education: Revised Imperatives," *Mountain/Plains Adult Education Journal*, Fall 1974, pp. 13–15.

Fuller, Jack. "Continuing Education by Objectives," *Journal of Continuing Education*, Dec. 1971, pp. 175–79.

Fuller, Jack. "Developing Community Leadership," *Community/Junior College Journal*, April 1975.

Fuller, Jack. "Educational Specifications for Building R," *William Rainey Harper College Master Plan*, 1974.

Fuller, Jack. "MBO Revisited," *Adult Leadership*, Sept. 1973, pp. 112–14.

Fuller, Jack. "Pass the Smart Pills, Please," *Perspective*, May 1974, p. 4.

Fuller, Jack. "Serving the Community Through Marketing and Management Seminars," *Journal of Business Education*, December 1972, pp. 117–20.

Fuller, Jack. "Simulation in a Political Science Classroom," *College and University Teaching*, Fall 1973, pp. 284–86.

Fuller, Jack. "Survey of Community College, Community Service Funding Patterns," William Rainey Harper College, unpublished study, Fall 1973.

Fuller, Jack. "Women's Programs," *Action*, Jan. 1971, p. 4.

Harlacher, E. *The Community Services Dimension of the Community College*. Englewood Cliffs, N.J.: Prentice-Hall, 1969.

Jacobson, Robert L. "Colleges Are Not Meeting Needs of Adults," *Chronicle of Higher Education*, Feb. 5, 1973, p. 6.

Jensen, G.; Liveright, A. A.; and Hallenbeck, W. *Adult Education*. Washington, D.C.: Adult Education Ass., 1964.

Jensen, Glenn. *Handbook of Adult Education*. London: Macmillan, 1970.

Johnson, S. R., and Johnson, R. B. *Developing Individualized Instructional Material*. Palo Alto: Westinghouse Learning Press, 1971.

Johnstone, J., and Rivera, R. *Volunteers for Learning*. Chicago: Aldine, 1965.

Lundsburg, David. "Community College Community Services: Rhetoric or Reality?" *Adult Leadership*, Dec. 1973, pp. 17–18.

Mager, Robert F. *Preparing Instructional Objectives*. Palo Alto, Calif.: Fearon Publishers, 1962.

Maltin, L. *Movie Comedy Teams*. New York: Signet, 1974.

"Most People Want to Learn More," *Saturday Review*, April 1973, pp. 23–24.

"Night School," *Newsweek*, March 5, 1973.

Odiorne, George S. *Management-by-Objectives*. New York: Pitman Publishing Co., 1965.

Olsson, David E. *Management by Objectives*. Palo Alto, Calif.: Pacific Books Publishers, 1968.

Planning Facilities to Accommodate Adult Education. Albany, N.Y.: State Education Department, Division of School Buildings and Grounds, 1958.

Ricklefs, R. "As Full-Time Enrollments Level Off, More Colleges Push Adult Education," *The Wall Street Journal,* Dec. 27, 1973.

Sheets, Wendell R., and Hostetler, Robert E. "How to Organize for EDSPECS Development," *Community and Junior College Journal,* April 1973, pp. 24–25.

Strub, G. F. "Adult Education Facilities," *The School Executive,* Nov. 1957, pp. 32–34.

Thornton, James W., Jr. *The Community College.* New York: John Wiley & Sons, 1966.

Index

JACK W. FULLER is a widely published authority in the field of continuing adult education and has administered such programs for a variety of institutions. The co-editor of *Career Education: A Life Long Process* (Nelson-Hall, 1978), Dr. Fuller's articles have appeared in such periodicals as *Journal of Business Education, Community/Junior College Journal* and *Community Education.* He is the present dean of Extended Day and Summer Programs at Pima Community College in Tucson, Arizona and has held a similar post at William Rainey Harper Community College in Palatine, Illinois. A member of numerous professional societies, he received his doctorate in education from the University of Wyoming.